HYMNING & HAWING ABOUT
AMERICA

HYMNING & HAWING ABOUT AMERICA

A FEW SYMBOL-MINDED ESSAYS

by FRANK TRIPPETT

Copyright © 2000 The Estate of Frank Trippett.
All rights reserved.

The NEWSWEEK essay was first published in NEWSWEEK Magazine. Copyright © 1964 NEWSWEEK, Inc. All rights reserved. Reprinted by permission.

All TIME essays were first published in TIME magazine. Copyright © 1977-1989 TIME Inc. All rights reserved. Reprinted by permission.

Jacket design and photographs Copyright © 2000 Robert Trippett. All rights reserved.

Library of Congress Number:		00-191076
ISBN #:	Hardcover	0-7388-2238-8
	Softcover	0-7388-2239-6

All rights reserved. No part of this book may be reproduced or transmitted in any form or by any means, electronic or mechanical, including photocopying, recording, or by any information storage and retrieval system, without permission in writing from the copyright owner.

This book was printed in the United States of America.

To order additional copies of this book, contact:
Xlibris Corporation
1-888-7-XLIBRIS
www.Xlibris.com
Orders@Xlibris.com

"Time passing as men pass
who will never come again
And leaving us, Great God,
with only this . . .
Knowing that this earth,
this time, this life,
are stranger than a dream."
—Thomas Wolfe

Frank Trippett's friends and fellow writers
Memorial Dedication,
THE NEW YORK TIMES, July 10, 1998

For Poppie,
who gave more love than tongue can tell.

Table of Contents

INTRODUCTION 8

ONE

A Season For Hymning And Hawing 12
The Ordeal Of Fun 16
What's Happening To Sexual Privacy? 30
Watching Out For Loaded Words 35
In Louisiana: Jazzman's Last Ride 39
The Suckers 44
Why There Is No Place Like It 59
Get This Season Off The Couch! 63

TWO

The Scientific Pursuit Of Happiness 68
Little Crimes Against "Nature" 74
Getting Dizzy By The Numbers 78
The Secret Life Of The Common Cold 82
The Weather: Everyone's Favorite Topic ... 86
The Great American Cooling Machine 91
A New Distrust Of The Experts 96
Living Happily Against The Odds 101

THREE

On Leading The Cheers For No. 1 106
The Human Need To Break Records 110
The Bull Market In Personal Secrets 114
There Must Be A Nicer Way 118

Hard Times For The Status-Minded 122
The Game Of The Name 126
Time To Reflect On Blah-Blah-Blah 131
So You Want To Be A Journalist 135

FOUR

A Few Symbol-Minded Questions 140
Why So Much Is Beyond Words 144
Slogan Power! Slogan Power! 149
Looking For Mr. President 153
The Trivial State Of The States 157
States' Rights And Other Myths 162
The Public Life Of Secrecy 169
Why Doesn't My Government
    Stop Lying To Me? 175
The Busting Of American Trust 184

FIVE

While America Slept:
    The Turbulent Peace Between The Wars .. 190
Some Cases Never Die, Or Even Fade 201
W.W. II: Present And Much Accounted For ... 205
The Marshall Plan: A Memory, A Beacon ... 212
An Account Of Some
    Conversations On U.S. 45 219
The South 226
The Hesse Trip 232
The '70s: A Time Of Pause 245
Looking For Tomorrow (And Tomorrow) 249

ABOUT THE AUTHOR 254

INTRODUCTION

Presidential campaigns remind me of Frank Trippett, because whenever one of them rolled around, Frank's friends used to ask him why he had lost the nomination again. A Mississippian, his answer was always: "Ah peaked too soon." That was a misfortune for the country. Frank, had he bothered to run, would have been one of the smartest, most right-minded, most good-hearted Presidents ever—certainly the funniest. The word "pretense" never came within a mile of him. On his first day of work at *NEWSWEEK*, he ran into the magazine's patrician managing editor, Osborne Elliott. Elliott introduced himself and extended his hand. "Oz Elliott," he said. Frank replied: "Ah's Trippett."

At *TIME*, to which he later moved, he was revered and loved by critics like Stefan Kanfer, and by his fellow essayists, Lance Morrow and myself. He was a type that was rare on the American scene—the Southern Democrat reporting on civil rights, whose sense of justice was especially acute for having been cultivated where injustice was once the law. Frank was also an individual. As these essays show, he had a stylish elegance; a calm capable of rage at the right moments; and a wit that could at once floor you and leave you smiling. In "So You Want To Be A Journalist," he identified the main purpose of punditry as providing "busy work and pasturage for resonant and well-connected journalists who have outgrown toil, prevalent realities, and teachability."

That never applied to Frank. He was not well-connected; he was disconnected. His journalism consisted simply of watching his country carefully and doing his work. He probably would have been a bit embarrassed by the idea of collecting and publishing his pieces, but that's all right. Thanks to this book, the rest of us may have the pleasure of the evidence of an exceptionally useful and valuable life. I only wish that reading these fine essays did not serve as a reminder that Frank is no longer next door.

Roger Rosenblatt
Editor-at-Large at TIME Inc.
March, 2000

ONE

A Season For Hymning And Hawing

The Ordeal Of Fun

What's Happening To Sexual Privacy?

Watching Out For Loaded Words

In Louisiana: Jazzman's Last Ride

The Suckers

Why There Is No Place Like It

Get This Season Off The Couch!

A Season For Hymning And Hawing

1977

Technically, it begins next week. Actually, it began with the epic sigh of relief that could be sensed all over the U.S. right after Labor Day. Even before it arrives, Americans always manage to get into autumn. And no wonder. It is easily the most habitable season of the year.

Indeed, autumn deserves a hymn—and it has received far less tribute than it deserves. True, some mixed notices have come in over the centuries. Horace slandered autumn as a "dread" period—"harvest-season of the Goddess of Death." He was dead wrong, of course, for as Ovid noted, once he got his mind off sex, autumn is "*cum formossisimus annus*"—"the fairest season of the year." Had he lived a little later, Horace might have found out from the U.S. Census Bureau that the death rate is usually lower in autumn than in winter and spring. Why? Science doesn't know, but it is quite possible that the will to live is stronger in the fall. Conversely, the will to mayhem weakens: nobody has ever worried about a Long Hot Autumn.

So autumn is a blatantly vital season, contrary to the allegations of sorrowful poets who misconstrue the message of dying leaves. A more realistic poet, Archibald MacLeish, says that "Autumn is the American season. In Europe the leaves turn yellow or brown and fall. Here they take fire on the trees and hang there flaming. Life, too, we think, is capable of taking fire in this country; of creating beauty never seen."

Autumn is also the authentic season of renewal. Yale Lecturer William Zinsser hit the nail squarely: "The whole notion of New Year's Day as the time of fresh starts and bold resolutions is false." In truth that time is autumn. Popular pleasure shows itself in those hastening steps and brightened smiles encountered as the air grows nippier. Some psychiatrists have patients who grow almost alarmed at how congenial they suddenly feel. Autumn is a friendlier time. The rejuvenating ambience of autumn is immeasurably more ancient than even the calendar. The Creation itself was achieved in the autumn, according to a tradition of Judaism—whence the Jewish New Year, Rosh Hashanah, at summer's end or the start of fall. The suspicion that even God is partial to autumn has overwhelmed others, including John Donne, who enthused: "In Heaven, it is always Autumn."

No, autumn is not always heaven on earth. The season does induce a quickening of the blood and a heightening of humankind's sensual pleasures. Yet the very jubilant excesses that ensue often lead, at last, to the well-known post-Thanksgiving "holiday blues." In darker ways still, fate and tragedy have made some American Novembers seem more cruel than April.

Autumn is honest, it does not pretend to be heaven. Yet almost everybody recognizes that the season's character transcends those familiar bracing days, crystal nights, bigger stars, vaulted skies, fluted twilights, harvest moons, frosted pumpkins and that riotous foliage that impels whole traffic jams of leaf freaks up into New England (even though Columnist Russell Baker has reminded them that "if you've seen 1 billion leaves, you've seen them all"). What is not widely recognized is that autumn is richly enhanced simply by what it is not. Specifically, it is not summer, winter or spring.

Take winter. It is basically uninhabitable. Whenever it shows its true nature, real life bogs to a standstill. Almost no one sincerely likes winter except the oil cartel and the cough-syrup magnates. True, everybody pretends that real life actually goes on. This very effort has inspired some of mankind's most desperate inventions—curling and skiing, to name two.

13

To help foster the illusion of life happening, the Constitution requires Congress to convene each January—and the illusion is sometimes convincing even if the Capitol is often the scene of more commotion than movement. Winter is, in a word, unacceptable.

Then there is spring, the season for simpering adolescents, May flies and impressionable poetasters. Listen to a typical springophile, Poet George Herbert: "Sweet Spring, full of sweet days and roses,/ A box where sweets compacted lie;/ My music shows . . ." Hold! Enough! His muse-ack provides sufficient cause to reflect—coolly—on the hard fact that spring was the time when our ancestral tribes built festivals around the rites of blood sacrifice. Moreover, did not Eve accomplish the Fall of Man in the eternal spring of Eden? In cool weather, serpents do not tempt; they grow diffident, recede and hibernate.

Summer? If any abomination so current needs to be reprised, think of it. Drought. Crowded beaches. Sunburn. Poison ivy. McDonald's. Summer is sand between the toes, fleafestations on the cats, movies like *New York, New York*. Every so-called joy of summer—whether getting wet, beering up or fleeing to the mountains—consists, in its essence, of *escaping* the suffocating reality of the season. August is so horrible that even dedicated psychiatrists abandon posts and patients for the entire month. Mosquitoes love summer. They hate autumn.

In short, winter is a tomb, spring is a lie, and summer is a pernicious mirage. Thus, if only by some crude law of relativity, autumn is the preferred stock of seasons. Autumn is the truth. It had to be autumn (unless the fabled apple fell unseasonably) that inspired Newton to discover the law of gravity. More books and most of the best come forth in the autumn. In theatrical circles, autumn is spoken of as *the* season. Autumn is for stamping on ripe grapes. Even now the vintners are prowling the prodigal vines.

No hymning—or hawing—in behalf of autumn should neglect to note that the coming season is a self-contained climactic cycle. It offers every weather—at its end, days icy enough for any sane person, and along the way, those indefinite Indian summers that put the real ones to shame. Fittingly enough, autumn delivers us to Christmas.

Admittedly, the season has imperfections. Yet even some of these—such as pro football and TV premieres—have become popular. On the other hand, autumn's few blemishes tend to be offset, for civilized folk, by that man-made miracle, the World Series. Maybe the saddest defect of autumn in America is the fact the country is so large that some regions do not get to experience it—Southern California, for one. Inhabitants of such deprived places should be encouraged to make-believe. That sort of thing comes easy to any folk not brought firmly back to earth once a year by a fall.

—*TIME*, September 19, 1977

The Ordeal Of Fun

1969

We are conceived in a moment of profound fun. This fact may not fix our destiny, but it strongly insinuates our complicity in some cosmic carnival. Fun becomes us. Born out of fun, we are born into it too. "Play begins with the child's . . . sensuous manipulation of his body . . . and the *fun* of it all is a very fleshly satisfaction," says Prof. Theodore Roszak. "There is a simple and immediate joyousness in the functions and capacities of the body simply for what they are: the body's knowledge and enjoyment of itself is the act of play."

As it begins existence, fun through the course of life becomes the basis for judging the quality of existence. One sees this in the words of a physician who recently discussed the issue of medicated survival: "George Bernard Shaw was full of fun at 90. He would have been worth resuscitating. Some people would not be worth resuscitating at 56."

We may argue that the very end of existence is fun too (even if the termination of existence is not). Plato so argued: "Man is made God's plaything, and that is the best part of him. Therefore every man and woman should live life accordingly . . . Life must be lived as play . . ."

America's political commitment to the pursuit of happiness extends at least a cousinly embrace to that Platonic ideal. And in the nation's actual behavior the notion of life as a fun-quest has burgeoned wildly. Notions of fun permeate the national psyche willy-nilly. One might persuasively contend that the Kennedy Administration enchanted Americans not so much by policy as by its capacity for fun. And today, Art Buchwald, humorously speculating that "being in power" is really Richard Nixon's idea of fun, is confirmed by the President himself. After his election, Nixon said: "Having lost a close one eight years ago . . . I can say this—winning's a lot more fun." Fun is all over the summit. Spiro T. Agnew on being Vice President: "The work is easier, and the fun is more fun." Postmaster General Winton Blount, denying a rumor that he planned to resign, offered this: "I've never had more fun in my life." Obviously, life at the top induces an emotion not alien to the bliss of a moppet in a sandbox.

Fun pervades the whole national character. Almost 20 years ago, the *Journal of Social Issues* discovered "The Emergence of Fun Morality" in America, concluding: "Fun, from having been suspect if not taboo, has tended to become obligatory." Now it should be added that Americans are on a fun-jag of almost incalculable dimensions. The previously "obligatory" quest shows signs of being a runaway national compulsion. In certain ways it smacks of an ordeal. But on it goes. At a paradoxical moment when the country seems obsessed with anger, the pursuit of fun is expanding in ever-longer, ever-quicker leaps. To measure the phenomenon is to flirt with infinitude; one survey says Americans went walking for fun some 1,030,000,000 times in a recent year. Our economic commitment to fun is staggering: The fun market stands close to $150 billion now, says such a house as Merrill Lynch, Pierce, Fenner & Smith, and they confidently forecast it will reach $250 billion by 1975, outrunning all the rest of the economy. Already the fun-quest has reshaped big segments of the society, turning field hands into busboys and meadows into rest-stop communities. Such signs hint that a full-blown Fun Culture is being born. To note this may be to agree with Billy Graham that there's a "mad pursuit of fun," but it is not to agree that "moral decadence" is here. After all, Americans see fun as divine. "What was de angels doin' up dere?"

asks a boy in *The Green Pastures*. "I suppose," answered the parson, "dey jest flew aroun' and had a good time."

The purpose here is not to denounce the American fun-quest. Granted, California mate-swapping may not be deemed the apex of rectitude. Still, Californians also committed some big share of those 467 million bike rides taken one recent year—and the incidence of hanky-panky on bikes seems at worst negligible. This suggests that in America's gluttonous appetite for fun there is at least a latent innocence. No nation that boasts 43.9 million amateur musicians is irredeemable even if it does contain 45 million bridge players. Forbearance is indicated. The purpose here, anyway, is not to deplore. It is to explore.

Americans drove roughly 350 billion miles last year in quest of fun. This tells much of the scope of the quest but nothing of its success. Similarly the fact that we spent some $14.5 billion on booze reveals an enormous effort to have fun but fails as an index of attainment. So it is with the idea of 3.5 million skiers spending $3.5 billion yearly. One is tempted to suppose unlimited ecstasy on the slopes—unless one heeds, say, the words of journalist Hal Bruno: "The closest thing to fun in skiing is taking off those hellish boots at the end of the day." One must thread a way carefully through the fun-scape.

Statistics may measure the fun-kick, but only eyeballs and ears and intuition can assess it. To disclose that some 500,000 play the ukelele hardly establishes that 500,000 savage breasts are being soothed.

Fun is a vaporous notion. Everyone knows what it means, yet it eludes definition. By habit we associate fun with "recreation." Still, on second thought, everyone sees the flaw in this. Fun simply does not keep regular hours. Most scholarly studies of the subject fall short precisely because they focus exclusively on *leisure:* man-at-play differentiated from man-at-work. While this convention serves the sociological method, it conceals the size of the force at work in mankind's fun-quest. Instincts that turn the weekend into a fiesta are not dead from 8 to 5 on weekdays. Philosophers such as Bertrand Russell who denounce man's "belief in the virtuousness of work" fail to comprehend perhaps the nature of man, certainly the nature of work. It often amounts to a game. In *Homo Ludens*, the definitive study of the play instinct, historian Johan Huizinga located innumerable "sporting elements" in the workaday world and concluded: "Business becomes play." Some businessmen confirm this overtly. Hawaii's multimillionaire Chinn Ho clings to a typical code. "Unless you make business a game," he says, "you may as well have an early retirement." Nor is the work-is-play concept limited to commerce. Novelist Jacquin (*Look to Your Geese*) Sanders often introduces himself with the commonplace: "Sanders is my name, writin's my game."

And what of the utterly tedious job? Some compensatory dynamic rescues fun-loving man from tedium. The dullest jobs induce the most spectacular fantasies. Although Hollywood ineptly conceived him to be a proofreader, Walter Mitty, whose profession James Thurber did not reveal, probably was an assistant accountant.

In any event *homo ludens* (Man the Playful) clearly holds sway over *homo sapiens*. "Instead of the saw: 'All is vanity,' says Huizinga, "the more positive conclusion forces itself upon us that 'all is play.'" The play instinct, as he sees it, spawns man's myths and rituals: "In myth and ritual the great instinctive forces of civilized life have their origin: law and order, commerce and profit, craft and art, poetry, wisdom and science. All are rooted in the primaeval soil of play."

So to explore only man-at-leisure is to end only half-grasping fun—and to underestimate the force of the play instinct. It is ubiquitous, present even in the strenuous dissent of today's young. "Rebellion," says psychologist Joyce Brothers, "is partly based on the urge to have fun." Hip editor Paul

Krassner and Yippie leader Abbie Hoffman confirmed this. Krassner: "For older people, fun might be canasta. For the young, it is making a revolution." Hoffman: "Fun is just getting banged, fighting in the streets and roasting pigs."

An axiom emerges: For man, fun is not only scratching where he itches, it is itching where he scratches. Fun takes such myriad forms it smacks of illusion. This is appropriate. Illusion means literally "in-play." We know what produces fun but often don't see why. A young couple had been ecstatically gleeful on a spinning, jolting amusement-park ride. Question: "Why is being spun around so much fun?" Answer: "Who knows?" In the U.S. a vast industry has developed specifically designed to spin people around. Amusement parks call themselves "funspots" today. There are about 1,605 of them in the U.S. and Canada. They occupy 4,609 square miles of land. They employ 90,900 people. Exclusive of land, they represent a $1.4 billion investment. Last year 385 million customers spent $794 million mainly to get spun around. Very few people seem to know why. One meets skiers, surfers, boatmen and kite-fliers equally at a loss to fathom the essential source of their fun. They know where to scratch but do not know why they itch.

One must do better than that to comprehend why Americans drove 350 billion miles last year looking for fun. We may snicker at this nation's 7,000 unicyclists. But a communal motoring jag that consists of some 160 million vacation trips, among other jaunts, and costs $30 billion or so—this must be reckoned with. Is fun this important? And if so, why? What is its essence? We are driven, among other places, back to the beginning. *Playboy*'s boss Hugh Hefner thinks that fun "doesn't come naturally to us." But he could not be more wrong. It comes at birth. We must look at the infant and recognize ourselves.

The infant lies there: apotheosis of fun. Life explodes within him, about him. Each squirm, sniff, gasp, kick and gape ignites some fresh sensation. Each tick of awareness smites him uniquely: a ceaseless flickering of primal dawns. Shapes, motions, colors swarm about. Existence is protean, a kaleidoscopic cocoon. Incomprehensible sounds storm about him, cooings, scrapings, squeakings. Aromas and stinks flood alternately. Internal flexings signal fathomless gastric pleasures: He burps and grins idiotically, he breaks wind and orbits invisible moons. Hourly, new things come into focus. Life hurtles into his brains not as a single world but a dazzling succession of new worlds. The essence of entering life is disequilibrium. The infant is hurled into the air: He opens grinning gums to the skies and issues an ecstatic gasp as he plummets. To be? To be is to be in disequilibrium, visually, physically, aurally, internally. Life comes thus, and the infant is in love with it. Shortly, to survive in society, he will stifle much of this unfettered joy. But all his fun-seeking life he will work at recovering it. Later, when he comes as close as an adult can to recapturing the dizzy totality of it all, he will speak of *falling* in love.

Disequilibrium—and that ineluctable tandem sensation, the sense of other worlds—this is the essence of fun, this the quarry of the human fun-quest. When he brought us "out of the cradle endlessly rocking" Walt Whitman divined this essence. The man who grasps it knows at once why an earth-spawned primate loves the rolling sea with its protean shapes. Despite a vast literature that makes a mystery of this love, its origin is not concealed. Man loves the sea for the same reason an infant loves being rocked. Life is disequilibrium. Stillness is death. Infants hear a curious little song that places them in a cradle rocking in a windy tree-top—and are strangely lulled even though the song brings them falling down cradle and all. Alarmist critics have suggested that such a lullaby as *Rock-A-Bye, Baby* might induce "insecurity." They could hardly be further from the mark. Disequilibrium is the very stuff of infantile joy. When older, children will seek

21

to recover it at an amusement park where technology has fashioned complex machines that produce nothing else whatsoever.

A cumbersome word, yet crucial, disequilibrium. We seek it in action and in repose, in soaring and cycling, in booze and pot. It is the epitome of childhood's durable toys: the swing, the seesaw, the kite, the hoop. Nursery rhymes evoke it: Jack and Jill come tumbling down, and so does London Bridge. In no other thing on this ever-spinning globe is disequilibrium so perfectly embodied as in the ball—and around no other object has man fashioned so many games, hundreds of them including croquet, bowling, tennis and jacks and not excluding marbles and snooker. In dancing we induce such dizzy elation that we could have danced all night. Yet even after a jag of sedentary fun we tell of having "had a ball." We can even have a ball merely listening: Music, sound in cunning disequilibrium, is the most reliable means of evoking other worlds that rock and roll.

Such is the nub of fun's mystique. How distant is the para-sailer rising in his diaper-like harness from the infant hurled aloft by his papa? In the invariably childish aura of a strip joint, what is the balding businessman seeking if not a moment's semblance of the unstrapped eroticism of infancy? Even if the snorkeler's eerie reefs and the ice-fisherman's crackling blue cosmos are more clearly other worlds, isn't it yet plain that the hunter, too, with his elation in blood, inhabits another world, one now vanished from history?

It may be found anywhere, even behind total passivity. The motionless yogi may depart this mundane world, but at least part of his joy comes from a subtle dizziness induced by deep breathing and an oversupply of oxygen. Moreover, the layman who is awed by the transported yogi ought to recall that nearly any American will describe a moment of rare fun as being "out of this world." Our vernacular confirms fun's essence at many a whimsical turn. A successful party "takes off," a funless one "falls flat." We call our best spirits "soaring," our best moments "high," and our most uninhibited fun-seekers "swingers." This last word has many meanings, of course, which lands us at a neat place to note that wordplay itself is least of our pleasures. It is a common experience to get fun from a pun; it induces that perverse disequilibrium known as a sinking sensation. Half a laugh is better than none.

We take fun where we can find it. We dive and turn somersaults, we skate and we scooter, we fly up in planes and jump out in parachutes. We surf ("It's a lot like smoking pot," says a young Californian) and we snorkel. After discovering a great reef of St. Croix, 24-year-old Michigander Janie Buffong wrote in her diary: "It was truly another world. I did not ever want to be a land creature again." Elation (the state of being elevated) may be had underwater no less than on a mountainside—and in innumerable ways in man's innumerable games. At a static, square bridge table, with 52 static cards, we find it in the manic oscillation of emotions that flows from the fall of the cards. Similarly, from the rise and fall of his chips come the fun of the gambler—although pathologists tell us that the true gambler's ultimate pleasure arrives by a most devious route. The true gambler seeks this: To lose everything, to be stripped of possessions, hence of responsibility—and so to be an infant again. Then, to the consternation of relatives who don't fathom what is happening, he manifests high and incongruous elation.

A tilted psyche leads the compulsive gambler along this tortuous route questioning what men universally seek in the fun-quest—the recovery of infantile joy. The quest sends man to his depth and his heights. As Norman Brown notes in *Life Against Death*, his study of Freud, the "play-element in culture" provides "a prima facie justification for the psychoanalytical doctrine of sublimation which views 'higher' cultural activities as substitutes for lost infantile pleasures."

23

To fathom the American fun-binge we must grasp the full power of the play instinct. One cannot easily overstate its role in human development. We are used to thinking of the sex instinct as all prevalent. The play instinct is more powerful, necessarily: It *includes* the sex drive. As well, it was a crucial factor in the development of man's thinking brain (the cortex). Here you are shunted briefly to Dr. A. T. W. Simeons, an English physician. He wrote a brilliant study of psychosomatic medicine called *Man's Presumptuous Brain*. Exploring the evolution of the human psyche with the shrewdest insight, he demonstrates how life in the trees gave our progenitors enormous advantages over groundbound mammals. On the ground creatures had hardly a moment to spare, no play except for the very young:

"In the trees there were none of these problems. Once a certain degree of cortical development had been reached, all vital needs could be fulfilled in a few short bursts of activity. During the rest of the time there was nothing of vital importance to be done. Yet a highly active brain compelled man's animal ancestors to perform some sort of activity . . .

"Here again the higher tree-living mammals made use of the trick of continuing into adult life a trait that had hitherto been a privilege of the very young. They continued to play during their whole lives. They raced up and down the branches, chased each other for the sheer fun of it; they swung in the tree-tops and learned to leap from one precarious hold to another regardless of the void below. They learned to adopt the sitting posture, which made their forelimbs free for grasping, scratching, hunting for fleas . . . or toying with morsels of food. Such activities . . . provided the best possible training for sensory acuity, all forms of advanced nervous control and muscular co-ordination. The ability to play skillfully may already at this early stage have been a powerful factor in sexual selection. The better players probably had better chances with the opposite sex, and so this trait was inherited with increasing frequency and rapidly perfected. In modern man," Dr. Simeons goes on "playfulness has gone to extremes. He plays from earliest infancy until he dies. It is only the nature of his toys which changes with the passage of years."

If modern American man is not going to extremes, he is surely going to some extremely interesting lengths. The funscape is a statistical banquet. In one vastly surveyed recent year, Americans went swimming 970 million times, played outdoor sports 929 million times (there being 26 million players of softball alone) and bicycled 467 million times. The incidence of picnicking (451 million), fishing (322 million) and camping (97 million) is equally impressive. One may pity the 100,000 practitioners of *Moo Duk Kwan Tang Soo Do* (as Korean karate is called), but one must sit up at the thought that in 1967 some 41 million Americans used about 8.3 million boats and spent some $3 billion at retail in doing so. Imagine it: 10 million golfers on 9,615 courses, 15,000 pigeon racers, 40 million kites sold, 18 million roller skaters, 200,000 squash players, 94,000 tennis courts, around 2,000 sporting goods *manufacturers*, 10 million horseshoe pitchers, 150,000 mountain climbers, $1 billion worth of movie tickets, 20 million sports shooters including 17 million hunters, $5 billion spent on TV sets, radios, phonos, tape gear and $1.2 billion spent on records. One cannot forget those funwalks, far more than a billion of them, and one wonders whether the Merrill Lynch researcher who estimated the fun market at $150 billion figured in the cost of shoe leather. One wonders, too, what portion of the $420,020,000 spent on headache remedies yearly should be ascribed to the fun-quest.

Even neglecting sex, roque, curling and boccie (as well as the folks around Ada, Okla., who chase jackrabbits in jeeps), the epic size of the American fun-quest stands proved. But is it, to use a phrase dear to our mercantile souls, paying off? Is it paying off, that is, in *fun*? There is a

25

widespread feeling that much of the time it is not. Some huge if uncertain fraction of the fun-quest is sensed to be a flop—producing *something*, perhaps, but plainly not fun.

This phenomenon has been noted by widely divergent observers. A while back, critic Walter Kerr chronicled *The Decline of Pleasure*, and very recently critic Alan Pryce-Jones wrote an essay describing something he called *The Rise of Unpleasure*. Singer Pearl Bailey thinks "man has lost joy in being himself," and a physician named Harry J. Johnson makes the same point in a new book called *Eat, Drink, Be Merry, and Live Longer*. "Millions of people no longer have the capacity to be 'merry,' " says Dr. Johnson, and Harvard psychiatrist Armand Nicholi senses that generally America's leisure-time pursuits are "neither meaningful nor gratifying." It may be predictable that Billy Graham believes Americans are "not having true pleasure," but Tiny Tim—of all people—sounds exactly like Graham on the subject: "We're having less fun than before," says Tiny Tim, "because our moral codes have been crushed." New York *Times* women's editor Charlotte Curtis finds mostly ennui among the rich: "They search for a vacation to get away from vacation. They leave Mexico to go to Sardinia because they're exhausted. They leave Sardinia to go to Paris because they're exhausted. And so on . . ." Georgetown University psychiatrist Leon Salzman had the whole society in mind when he said: "Fun has become a bigger chore . . . a burden."

Somewhere, obviously, the fun-quest fails. Still, such observations should not come as news to any American who keeps his ears open. In our folklore the phenomenon of Blue Monday springs not from the premise that the worker's burden is heavier as the week begins but from the presumption that he will be exhausted from a weekend of play. Fun, of course, does not exhaust, it refreshes. Yet, another striking modern folk tradition all but obliges an American to return from a vacation not refreshed, as after fun, but feeling like hell, as after an ordeal. The pity is that most of the time we do not have to fake this feeling. Most of the time the fun-quest has worn us out as though it were an ordeal.

Our recent way of explaining this has been to imagine the American to be in some way incapable of fun—even though anybody can think of exceptions enough to shatter this notion to bits. Nevertheless it has long been faddish to presume that he is burdened still by the old Puritan credo. Hugh Hefner speaks of our "Puritan hang-up" and Joyce Brothers chimes in with "the Puritan ethic is still prevalent." Such diagnoses fail, however. They lead us down a false path. They suggest that our former prohibitions on fun were "moral" and that our "unpleasure" today results from that lingering morality. This diagnosis proceeds from a flaw—the failure to see that the Puritan ethic was not "moral" at all but economic. In the Puritan's day, when every living hand was needed to shuck the corn or pick the flax, fun-seeking was a "sin" because it jeopardized the community's economic survival. Preachers like the Rev. Hugh Peter of Salem, who harangued against loafing ("An hour's idleness is as bad as an hour's drunkenness"), simply wove a tissue of morality around the economic facts of life. The old phrase "root, hog, or die" reveals how the settlers really felt about the loafer. Today, of course, the fun-seeker is universally applauded. But this is not because it is now moral where it was once immoral. This is because it is now profitable where it was once unprofitable.

Fun has become a consumer product. Here I should say "fun"—quote unquote. Fun remains what we know it to be. "Fun" is the consumer product. "Fun" is hucksterered in a glittering package. When the package proves empty, Americans are understandably crushed. This country's soul was shaped more by the mercantile spirit than the Puritan morality. It is hard to prove even vestigial Puritanism in a folk who are not only on a $150 billion fun-kick but widely suspected of sexual profligacy as well. But we know clearly how the American behaves when he has been sold a bill of goods. And what is the essence of "fun," the consumer product? Most often it is the emptiness of—*elsewhere*.

So we return at last to those 350 billion miles we drove last year in quest of "fun." Why did we so compulsively believe that fun was *elsewhere*? Why did we elect to travel so feverishly at precisely the time when there are fewer differences to see in the country, at a time when a vacation motel in Ft. Pierce or Duluth is exactly like the one in Phoenix? What persuades us that half the "fun" is in the *going*? Why do we remain enamored of the "joy of the open road" when bumper-to-bumper life is identical on the New Jersey Turnpike or the Santa Barbara Freeway? What drives us on and on and on and on—*elsewhere* questing "fun"?

Truth shouts at us from every TV screen, it comes with lilting music urging us up, up and away; it calls out from every four-color auto ad. The same technology that turned us into a nation-on-wheels is fashioning the new "fun" culture. It applauds the long-distance "fun" seeker in a ceaseless deluge of hypnotic ads. The technology spent more than $214 million last year advertizing travel alone. It spent $675 million hawking automobiles in ads invariably designed to trigger the powerful play instinct. In a thousand cunning ways, the ads say *go* and you will find "fun"—*elsewhere*. In our more lucid moment we all know the reality that lies along the grinding turnpike as we know the reality that lies at the end of the line. It is easy *elsewhere* to find a restaurant exactly like the one down the road from your house. But that "fun" that they told you about? It often turns out like the "whiter-than-white" detergent ingredient, existing only as a fantasy in a huckster's mind. So Americans are discovering again and again an ancient truth: You may find fun *elsewhere*—but only the fun you bring with you. For that, as every child knows, is where it is at.

In *The Bacchants,* Euripides told how the citizens of Thebes were being inveigled afar by the notion of guaranteed fun—bacchic revels that sounded juicy but turned into ash. At one point Euripides brings on the chorus to . . . Hey, Eurip! Bring on the chorus:

If man, in his brief moment, goes after things too great for him, he may lose the joys within his reach. To my mind, this is the way of madness and perversity.

Trite? True. True? Quite. Have fun. Go, go, go. Up, up and awry.

—*LOOK,* July 29, 1969

What's Happening To Sexual Privacy?

1970

Our times surely must become known as the Age of the Great Disrobing. Public sex pops up everywhere. Across an ever-expanding vista we behold natural rites hitherto closed off by an ancient rule of privacy. Now we witness it all—at the movies, in published stills, in the cool, bare cavortings of the young at play. Clearly, privacy is steadily passing.

So far this phenomenon has been more eloquently decried than explained. Here I wish neither to mourn the old custom nor inflame the social anxiety induced by its waning. Self-understanding is the best therapy for anxiety, and to this end I take up this subject. To allay futile fear we need to grasp the reason why the rule of sexual privacy is vanishing. I offer an answer.

First we must divine why we invented this rule. So I invite you to the wildwood, where we lived before our evolving mind impelled us to the dawn of what the anthropologist calls culture. Back then, we performed the act of procreation in the way of any other mammal. Irrepressible instinct impelled us as it did the lion, the monkey, the mastodon. We mated to perpetuate life, wherever instinct and opportunity coincided—as indifferent to the eyes of our tribesmen as would be wolves to the gaze of their lurking pack mates.

We hid not from fellow men but from other predatory beasts. Among our own we needed no privacy. Such a need is not instinctual. It is still not experienced by other mammals with instinctual mechanisms just like our own. They may hide for safety while mating. They have no need to hide from each other.

We, of course, departed from this practice of open sexual engagement. Our deviation came as a consequence of the peculiar way that our brain evolved. Our brain started out as a rudimentary apparatus, a mechanism that responded to sensory perceptions and sensations by triggering the physiological reactions appropriate to fear, rage, hunger and the sex drive—all the instincts that a mammal needs to sustain, protect and perpetuate the life of its species.

This primitive instinctual mechanism is, in truth, still with us, still functions. It operates beyond the direct reach of consciousness in that nether region of the brain called the diencephalon, the "brain stem." Signals from the diencephalon still cause us to know fear, anger, hunger, lust. But today we screen and censor and modify these instincts through the elaborate mechanisms of our cortical brain—the cortex.

Students are fond of comparing the cortex to a computer. It stores information, recalls it, sorts it. It controls—or seems to control—many of our conscious functions. Long ago, we did not possess this remarkable part of our brain. It grew over a vast period of time. Finally it gave us a capacity not present in other mammals. It gave us that super-recall known as memory, and that super-consciousness known as imagination. These unique capacities eventually obliged us to adopt the rule of sexual concealment. It was spawned as an expedient that directly served our survival.

The fantastic development of the cortical brain, of course, impelled us into culture through its inventiveness, its power of imagination, its capacity to conceive as potentially actual things not yet actually existing. This same capacity, for better or worse, dictated the end of unconcealed sexual engagement. We had to submit to the suppression of many natural and individual tendencies to survive and perpetuate ourselves as creatures of culture. As we reached the dawn of culture, our survival required, among other things, certain economic coordinations not previously known on earth. There were tribal migrations, the need for group flight from certain natural enemies and menacing climatic conditions. When fire became a tool, there was a need to nurture and tend it. Eventually we knew a need to manufacture other tools. Facing such needs, we discovered—gradually, no doubt—that visible sexual engagements among us tended to be a social liability. This, though I doubt we pondered it at the time, was due to our unique gifts of memory and imagination.

Obviously, these capacities make us susceptible to stimulation to a degree not known among other mammals. In the absence of direct stimulation, others can witness the procreative act with utter detachment. A rhinoceros, if shown a picture of two rhinoceroses mating, will display no interest whatever. Unless the wind is just right, the rhinoceros will remain similarly indifferent if witnessing two actual rhinoceroses mating. We are not like that. Our imagination tends to project us into the act that we are witnessing. Imagination thus stimulates us as would an actual sexual scent or contact. This is well known to our vast pornography industry. This susceptibility also provides the incentive for today's widespread orgies. One consequence of this peculiar susceptibility is that visible sex long ago tended to thwart new cultural imperatives.

Imagine, if you will, the effect on a forced migration if Awg and Mug locked themselves in the procreative act by the wayside, inducing an epidemic of instinctual lust. Life might have ended not with a whimper but a bang. Or imagine the effect on certain economic activities of unconcealed sexual engagement when this mode overlapped the beginnings of culture.

There hunkers the tribe. Our Big Man has set Oog the Flint Chipper to chipping flint. Oog starts chipping. Soon he glances up and sees Awg and Mug making it ten feet away. Instantly Oog's imagination dispels all interest in flint production. He drops his flint and trots away to drag Ung out of the cave. Suddenly the Big Man looks around to discover—well, there they go again.

Being himself a warm-blooded mammal he at first entertains no thought of disapproving. Living through innumerable repetitions of this, however, the Big Man eventually gropes his way to the conclusion that since the tribe needs flint chipped if it is to survive, something must be done. Finally he suggests that Awg and Mug go off in the bushes if mate they must during flint-chipping time. Right here the concept of sexual privacy is born.

No doubt a long succession of Big Men, tribal leaders, discovered that simple political directives would not suffice to suppress our exceedingly powerful procreative drive. So gradually coercion was reinforced by a web of magical and religious taboos, and these more or less worked. They are still more or less in force, of course. This web of ancient taboos and prohibitions and commandments emerges today in the form of those diverse moral strictures that form our conscious rationalization of the rule of sexual privacy.

Just so was born the rule we see so clearly waning today. We do not so clearly see why it is waning. Most fundamentally, it is because our real need for the rule is waning. Less and less does the ancient custom serve the survival of the species. Our technological civilization, far from being disrupted by the practice of public sex, is engendering this phenomenon.

As technology increasingly depersonalizes and dehumanizes our lives, it is spawning in us a need to reassert that which is most basic and vital in us, our instincts. Moreover, technology is sweeping us into an epoch when privacy is becoming quite literally impossible. It will become impossible, on one hand, because of sheer population density, and, on the other, because of rapidly advancing technical means of surveillance in a civilization whose societies obviously intend to keep all individuals under constant watch.

One paramount need thus is dawning: the need to dwell, more or less as human beings, in a society in which privacy is out of the question. Our answer apparently is going to be to adopt a mode of life in which privacy is no longer considered necessary. So I suspect that public sex should be seen as the wave of our future just as it must be seen as the tide of our innocent past.

—LOOK, October 20, 1970

Watching Out For Loaded Words

1982

Via eye and ear, words beyond numbering zip into the mind and flash a dizzy variety of meaning into the mysterious circuits of knowing. A great many of them bring along not only their meanings but some extra freight—a load of judgment or bias that plays upon the emotions instead of lighting up the understanding. These words deserve careful handling—and minding. They are loaded.

Such words babble up in all corners of society, wherever anybody is ax-grinding, arm-twisting, back-scratching, sweet-talking. Political blather leans sharply to words (*peace, prosperity*) whose moving powers outweigh exact meanings. Merchandising depends on adjectives (*new, improved*) that must be continually recharged with notions that entice people to buy. In casual conversation, emotional stuffing is lent to words by inflection and gesture: the innocent phrase, "Thanks a lot," is frequently a vehicle for heaping servings of irritation. Traffic in opinion-heavy language is universal simply because most people, as C.S. Lewis puts it, are "more anxious to express their approval and disapproval of things than to describe them."

The trouble with loaded words is that they tend to short-circuit thought. While they may describe something, they simultaneously try to seduce the mind into accepting a prefabricated opinion about the something described. The effect of one laden term was incidentally measured in a recent survey of public attitudes by the Federal Advisory Commission on Intergovernmental Relations. The survey found that many more Americans favor governmental help for the poor when the programs are called "aid to the needy" than when they are labeled "public welfare." And that does not mean merely that some citizens prefer H_2O to water. In fact, the finding spotlights the direct influence of the antipathy that has accumulated around the benign word *welfare*.

Every word hauls some basic cargo or else can be shrugged aside as vacant sound. Indeed, almost any word can, in some use, take on that extra baggage of bias or sentiment that makes for the truly manipulative word. Even the pronoun *it* becomes one when employed to report, say, that somebody has what *it* takes. So does the preposition *in* when used to establish, perhaps, that zucchini quiche is *in* this year: used just so, *in* all but sweats with class bias. The emotion-heavy words that are easiest to spot are epithets and endearments: *blockhead, scumbum, heel, sweet-heart, darling, great human being* and the like. All such terms are so full of prejudice and sentiment that S.I. Hayakawa, a semanticist before he became California's U.S. Senator, calls them "snarl-words and purr-words."

Not all artfully biased terms have been honored with formal labels. Word loading, after all, is not a recognized scholarly discipline, merely a folk art. Propagandists and advertising copywriters may turn it into a polished low art, but it is usually practiced—and witnessed—without a great deal of deliberation. The typical person, as Hayakawa says in *Language in Thought and Action*, "takes words as much for granted as the air."

Actually, it does not take much special skill to add emotional baggage to a word. Almost any noun can be infused with skepticism and doubt through the use of the word *so-called*. Thus a friend in disfavor can become a *so-called friend*, and similarly the nation's leaders can become *so-called leaders*. Many other words can be handily tilted by shortening, by prefixes and suffixes, by the reduction of formal to familiar forms. The word *politician*, which may carry enough downbeat connotation for most tastes, can be given additional unsavoriness by truncation: *pol.* By prefacing liberal and conservative with *ultra* or *arch*, both labels can be saddled with suggestions of inflexible fanaticism. To speak of a pacifist or peacemaker as a *peacenik* is, through a single syllable, to smear someone with the suspicion that he has alien loyalties. The antifeminist who wishes for his (or her) prejudice to go piggyback on his (or her) language will tend to speak not of feminists but of *fem-libbers.* People with only limited commitments to environmental preservation will tend similarly to allude not to environmentalists but to *eco-freaks.*

Words can be impregnated with feeling by oversimplification. People who oppose all abortions distort the position of those favoring freedom of private choice by calling them *pro-abortion.* And many a progressive or idealist has experienced the perplexity of defending himself against one of the most peculiar of all disparaging terms, *do-gooder.* By usage in special contexts, the most improbable words can be infused with extraneous meaning. To speak of the "truly needy" as the Administration habitually does is gradually to plant the notion that the unmodified *needy* are falsely so. Movie Critic Vincent Canby has noticed that the word *film* has become imbued with a good deal of snootiness that is not to be found in the word *movie. Moderate* is highly susceptible to coloring in many different ways, always by the fervid partisans of some cause: Adlai Stevenson, once accused of being too *moderate* on civil rights, wondered whether anyone wished him to be, instead, immoderate.

The use of emotional vocabularies is not invariably a dubious practice. In the first place, words do not always get loaded by sinister design or even deliberately. In the second, that sort of language is not exploited only for mischievous ends. The American verities feature words—*liberty, equality*—that, on top of their formal definitions, are verily packed with the sentiments that cement U.S. society. The affectionate banalities

37

of friendship and neighborliness similarly facilitate the human ties that bind and support. The moving vocabularies of patriotism and friendship are also subject to misuse, of course, but such derelictions are usually easy to recognize as demagoguery or hypocrisy.

The abuse and careless use of language have been going on for a long time: witness the stern biblical warnings such as the one in *Matthew 12: 36*: "Every idle word that men shall speak, they shall give account thereof in the day of judgment." Yet the risks of biased words to the unwary must be greater today, in an epoch of propagandizing amplified by mass communications. "Never," Aldous Huxley said, "have misused words—those hideously efficient tools of all the tyrants, warmongers, persecutors and heresy hunters—been so widely and disastrously influential." In the two decades since that warning, the practice of bamboozlement has, if anything, increased. The appropriate response is not a hopeless effort to cleanse the world of seductive words. Simple awareness of how frequently and variously they are loaded reduces the chances that one will fall out of touch with so-called reality.

—TIME, May 24, 1982

In Louisiana: Jazzman's Last Ride

1981

Boom! A cannon shot from the Society Jazz Band bass drum jolts the chattering crowd outside the Gertrude Geddes Willis Funeral Home into a brief silence. The casket is coming out. *Boom!* A second shot signals the stricken cadence of a dirge. The white gloves of the pallbearers flash in the morning sun as they float their burden to the silver-gray Cadillac hearse. The main party of mourners, a score or so, fit themselves into several cars waiting in line.

Boom! Boom!

A cornet sings out the opening tones of a familiar old hymn. Quickly, other voices surge forth, trombones, saxophones, a beseeching clarinet, trumpets, tubas. The sound of *Just a Closer Walk with Thee* throbs across the leafy neighborhood of rundown houses, gas stations, union hall, stores and churches. It is late in the year, but the weather is soft. Just above, on the elevated expressway, traffic whips by, but on the ground the slow beat of the music warps the day's rhythm into a doleful sway.

A jazz funeral is beginning in New Orleans. Though hardly disrespectful, the underlying temper is festive. The reason lies in tradition: when the funeral is done, the streets will explode with jubilant jazz and antic celebration. To see it is to understand what Trumpeter Willie Pajaud meant when he said: "I'd rather play a funeral than eat a turkey dinner."

In New Orleans as far back as memory runs, marching brass bands have always tried to spread a bit of joy after the sorrow of a burial. Every jazz giant in the New Orleans pantheon—Kid Ory, Jelly Roll Morton, Bunk Johnson—developed his art partly by playing for funerals. The king of them all, Louis Armstrong, played a funeral the very day in 1922 when a telegram sent him off to join King Oliver in Chicago and soon onward to world fame.

Years later, in the record *New Orleans Function,* Armstrong recalled the traditional funeral by using *Flee as a Bird* as the processional dirge, *Didn't He Ramble* as a sample of swinging postburial music and an affectionate spoof of graveside eulogy. Says the Rev. Satchmo: "Ashes to ashes/ Dust to dust/ It's too bad old Gate/ Couldn't have stayed on earth with us." Armstrong never referred to a jazz funeral. Those who have nurtured the tradition speak simply of a funeral "with a band of music." Given New Orleans' love for parades, the outcome, however, is the same—and perhaps inevitable. A musical funeral procession always attracts a crowd much bigger than the main body of mourners, and it is this public aggregation, known as "the second line," that surrenders to a carnival spirit after the band "turns the body loose" (as the musicians put it), and on the homeward march begins rocking the air with solid jive.

The man being laid to rest today was himself a jazzman. Albert Walters was his name. His melodic cornet was heard around town for more than half a century—and is still to be heard on such records as *Albert Walters with the Society Jazz Band* and *West Indies Blues.* Walters taught himself piano as a kid, took up the horn in 1927. He liked to say he was a carpenter by trade but a musician by choice. He appeared now and then with other traditionalists in Preservation Hall, but mostly he worked with Society Jazz. A short, stocky man, widowed several years ago, Walters retired from carpentering but never thought of quitting music. In fact, he had just had his horn reconditioned when he died of a heart attack at 75.

Albert Walters and his cornet took part in countless jazz funerals over the years. Now that his time has come, he is fondly remembered at his own funeral. The voice of English-born Drummer Andrew Hall, leader of Society Jazz: "You know his music had real feeling. He was funny too. He used to stick his finger in his ears while he was playing to check intonation. Said he could hear himself better that way." Tenor Saxophonist Teddy Johnson: "He was always ready for a laugh, always joking, making up nicknames for people. I called him Big Chief." There is wordless comment in the fact that musicians from not only Society Jazz but several other bands (Olympia, Tuxedo) have turned out to make sure that one of their own gets a fitting send-off.

Now a procession forms that fills up two lanes of spacious St. Bernard Avenue. The musicians, a dozen, whose numbers will grow with late arrivals, make a loose formation. The second-liners—young and old, black and white, genteel and funky, sober and not entirely so—press in upon the band's flanks, spill onto the sidewalks, straggle across the avenue's landscaped divider. Leading it all is a stately, gray-haired man in a frock coat and a silvered, tasseled sash, a spangled umbrella furled under his arm, a top hat held over his heart; and, alongside him, a shorter man, similarly gray and with similar bearing and similar attire. Thanks to confusion resulting from the mix of bands, the procession has wound up with two grand marshals. ("Albert would have laughed at that," Teddy Johnson says later.) Yet the two move as one: in perfect time with the cadence, each meticulously executes a gravely swaying strut. They are undistracted by whimsical second-liners who invade the street to emulate their not quite imitable style.

Boom! Boom!

The procession creeps forward, passing the squat, faded hall of Hod Carriers Local Union 153, a one-story commercial social center (AVAILABLE FOR ANY OCCASION), the New Bethel Missionary Baptist Church, white with green trim. *Lead Me, Savior* has followed *Just a Closer Walk with Thee,* and soon the dirge is *What a Friend We Have in Jesus.* The band is taking up *The Old Rugged Cross* as it comes to a halt under some towering live oaks: the front yard of Corpus Christi Catholic Church.

The deep church bell tolls. The casket passes into the decorous stillness of the vaulted interior, leaving the hundred or so second liners and the musicians outside. The organ plays hymns that would be favorites in any Baptist church: *In the Garden, Just as I Am*. A priest reads from Job and speaks of the "gift of music" that Albert Walters had. Funerals like Walters', as William J. Schafer fairly puts it in *Brass Bands and New Orleans Jazz*, are "public acts, theatrical displays designed not to hide burial as a fearful obscenity but to exhibit it as a community act." And the public's participation afterward is "a celebration of life as much as a recognition of the triumph of death."

Boom! As soon as the casket emerges, a bass drum shot shatters the air. The dirge-playing band leads the way up the road toward the cemetery, then separates from the casket. At first it retraces its route by drumbeat alone. Then the trumpet screams forth, the drummers swing out, belted choruses of *The Second Line* assail the sky. The crowd, most of it, becomes a blur of fidgeting feet, twisting torsos, bobbing heads. A corpulent man in an orange shirt spins and dips. An elderly woman executes a scampering step with the help of her cane. An open-shirted youth leaps to the hood of a car and, after a flurry of steps, floats down to earth without breaking his rhythm. Here and there gaudy umbrellas twirl in the air. Faces gleam with sweat and exuberance.

The scene becomes a moil of solo showing off, a gleeful choreographic cadenza that no choreographer could plot. All movement is as spontaneous as the music, which soon rides into *Going to the Mardis Gras* and, at last, into the tune that seems to be everybody's great expectation: *When the Saints Go Marching In*. A young woman in frayed jeans curves backward, in an affront to gravity, all the while clapping her hands, rending the air with throaty singing—"Oh, when the saints . . ." At times such carryings-on have been known to get out of hand.

But not today. In half an hour it is over—except for the receding ripples of laughter and neighborly joshing. The musicians mosey by twos and threes toward their cars at the hall. For a moment it is hard to remember the funeral that must by now have ended at the distant cemetery. It is easy, however, to remember Albert Walters. If his days on earth had even a dash of the style of his leaving it, he was no man to be pitied.

—*TIME*, April 20, 1981

The Suckers

1970

> To avoid misunderstandings: not everyone who gambles is a gambler... The gambler seeks and enjoys an enigmatic thrill which cannot be logically explained, since it is compounded of as much pain as pleasure.
> —Dr. Edmund Bergler,
> *The Psychology of Gambling*

Gamblers all, they ducked out of a hard rain that fell on Manhattan's fresh spring grime, and they rose up seven floors to a rented lodge room, straggling in, slumping helter-skelter in theater-type seats ranked along three walls, gradually filling the room with raucous, comradely bombast. They fell silent as a leader diffidently installed himself, a squat man, bouncy, with berry eyes plugged into a sagging face that bobbed up like a tragicomic float out of the sea of his vivid blue shirt. A rose-colored necktie spewed up in a ski jump over his pendulant belly. He was a gambler, too, and he reminded them of why they were there—to exit this thing that had ruled their lives, to arrest it, to be free.

The leader moored himself a hospitable distance from the lectern they all faced, a gaggle of salesmen and cabbies and businessmen, a doctor, a lawyer, a postman, a dozen as it began, growing to more than a score as others straggled in, shaking off the rain. Soon, berry eyes began signaling them up to the lectern, one by one, and there they uttered certain simple truths about themselves, or tried, Bernie and Bill and Arthur and Allan and Irving and Sam, disgorging poignant shreds of tattered lives.

In voices of grit and gravel they talked, staccato ones, hoarse ones, some ripped at the grammatical seams, turning t's into d's, some gutsy and profane, some brittle with anger, some crushed with anguish, some poised, practiced, restrained. They talked about gambling, and deep into the night I listened to voices that scarcely mentioned such things as cards and dice and horses. Gambling seemed an abstract rite, as they spoke of it, severed from apparatus, remote from any habitat.

Gambling was just an awful need, strange, inexplicable, irresistible, an urgent need by which each had been driven as by a quenchless thirst. It compelled them, in short, and turned life to a singular hell, a spiraling and pell-mell existence. It induced an experience so intense that it displaced all other feelings, gambling did, and the quest of it became a ceaseless chase, and often sleepless, a frantic, accelerating race to fuel a yearning that by its very nature assured an ever-diminishing supply of the money needed for fuel.

They had finagled, embezzled, stolen. They had borrowed, too, whatever could be borrowed at whatever interest, and they had ensnarled themselves in cunning tangles of kited checks and epic debts, and they had sweated out the grisly coercions of shylocks and various other single-minded creditors.

"One night, I found myself in a car with two guns pressed against my head." A young man spoke, a profane cat encased in tight trousers and scimitar-shaped sideburns.

They talked about gambling, but much else, of lives they had led and—poignantly—of those they had not. One told of "utter isolation." Another had lived "in a shell." One ran from a father to avoid getting beaten. To an emaciated scrap of a man had come word long ago of his wife's death, a telegram that reached him afar: "I didn't do nothing when I got it. I didn't send word on what to do with the children, no instructions, no 'I'm sorry,' no nothing. Fifteen minutes later, I was in

45

a card game." Tears burst out of squinched eyes, tumbling onto pale, cadaverous cheeks as he reeled away from the lectern.

Gambler followed gambler. In many an elliptical memory I heard a recurring plaint, unstated, submerged, but roiling near the surface. Finally one man found the words for it. He was short and pudging, neatly swathed in a blue blazer and a bright-yellow shirt, and to us all he said this:

"There is a tremendous gap between the pain that we suffered and the understanding that we have of it. We talk about those awful years that are behind us, of borrowing money and stealing and embezzling, of living day by day behind a facade. But what we really think about is this—we think of the love we lost and the love we were unable to find and the love we were unable to give."

Like morning sunshine these words fell upon me. They lit up the dark woods of the gambler's secret world like no others I had heard. I had listened to millions by then, I guess, and read thousands. For weeks I had browsed the gambler's inner world, hoping to explain him. To that session of Gamblers Anonymous, I had carried the weight of a burgeoning theory. Now suddenly it made sense. I felt like a pilgrim come home. It had been, as a matter of personal fact, a pilgrimage begun reluctantly.

I reject the view that life is a gamble, and early rid my mind of the postulate that life should be pursued as a competition, a race. Race with whom? For what? What prize out valued the life spent chasing it? Life itself was the prize—unsurpassable, given me, not won. To broach it as though it consisted of winning or losing seemed lunacy, a chase after some will-o'-the-wisp.

Thus biased, I early found gambling a pallid experience. Dice do not move me. Cards, riffle-splat, glaze my sensibilities, ennui. I have endured a few poker games only by getting drunk enough to avoid hearing the same joke over and over. "Winners laugh and joke, losers cry 'deal!'" Poker players ought to learn two jokes, like bridge players. Sports events strike me as epic waste. My occasional infantile yen for sports thrills I gratify by reciting the numbers 21-20 or 7-6—breathtaking scores whatever might have been the game. Horses are OK—as transportation.

So disposed, I scarcely imagined I would ever be called to a pilgrimage into the gambler's world. Of gambling I knew only common lore. It was big. Estimates of all wagering resembled the GNP. Horseplayers bet $5.3 billion *legally* in 1968, but bookies abounded. Maybe Americans wagered $200 billion last year. I didn't know. Nobody did. John Scarne, everybody's expert, said craps was the biggest game going, then poker, next horses. Like everyone, I had heard that casinos were proliferating in Nevada, in the islands, the Bahamas, the Caribbean. States like New York and New Hampshire had created legal fund-raising lotteries, others were talking them.

Gamblers? I had read about Dostoevsky, a chronic who felt he got his kick from losing, and about Nick the Greek, dying broke or nearly so, having said that if he could not play and win he would choose to play and lose. Psychiatry, I knew, was split several ways on what gambling really amounted to. Freudians inevitably saw in the rites of gambling the enactment of buried sexual wishes. Others suspected psychic-masochism at work, losses giving submerged pleasure to the pain-lover. Losing, some theorized, was a gambler's self-punishment for buried guilt. As for Dostoevsky, Freud himself seemed to suspect that by wishing to win, the novelist was swiving his mother, and, by going on to lose, punished himself for the incest. Farfetched, this seemed, but I was willing to weigh any guesswork at the start. Now, however, I have a view of my own.

Expertise I had not. True, I glimpsed one face of gambling in late youth. With my only brother (whom, to protect the innocent, I shall call Bernard), I ran a football parlay card my last college year. "T 'N' T GRID PIX," we called it, celebrating at once our identity and sense of power. I hustled them the season of 1946, the biggest game of which, Army-Notre Dame, ended 0-0, a tie that wiped out every card the suckers had bet on. After that, we folded, rich, and I never thought earnestly again about either gambling or football. The one lesson I took away that semester is that when you are gambling for the gambling establishment you simply are not gambling.

I growled with distaste at the prospect of spending part of my life around beings who spend *their* time on earth watching dice roll, cards fall and sports scores get posted. That is not what Yeats and I call plucking the golden apples of the sun. My prejudice ran deep. Yet, now I'm glad I did it, now that I know that gambling has almost nothing to do with cards and dice and scores. It is simply a means of engineering certain strange and compelling emotions. Those tools—the paraphernalia, the rules, the conventions, the odds, even the money, the betting stakes, the fuel—are as distinct from this phenomenon as is, say, a shovel from the hole it has dug. It was nice to know I would be writing not of the mumbo jumbo of odds and systems but of human beings, a love story of sorts.

Not all human beings (though it is smart to assert that *everybody* gambles) are gamblers. I must steal the word for my say, and shrink it to a tighter circle. My gambler is a compulsive, of which there may be some six million, or a chronic, of which there are probably more—all those in whom the act of gambling triggers substantial emotions, a compelling thing that tends to shape the life of the one who knows it and needs it. If you casually bet, and occasionally, you are not my gambler, nor if you bet only what you can afford. "If the loss won't hurt, it's not gambling," my gambler says. Put a painless dollar on a number, and you are buying a pipe dream, not gambling. I'll give the word back to the vernacular, now the pilgrimage is done.

That reluctant pilgrimage: A surlier man might have rejected the call. I finally took it as providential—and promptly projected trips to Puerto Rico, the Bahamas, Miami (though pained to leave New York's squalid sludge and ice), to New Orleans, Los Angeles, San Francisco, Monte Carlo, London, Hong Kong—a wistful plan curtailed by someone up there. I got as far as San Francisco, where there are Olympia oysters, great Muzak and a casino that uses only play money. Thence back to New York's clotted canyons.

Painfully, I sandwiched in Las Vegas, a locale I wished entirely to avoid merely because I had heard about it. Now I know it should be seen—not seen, really, but experienced, like a surreal dream. A writer should not report on that place: he should review it; its gloomy, womby gaming rooms, swarming with phantoms behind doughy masks, should be reviewed, like a Fellini film. They say that Fellini, just to provide lip movements onto which he later dubbed dialogue, obliged the actors in his *Satyricon* to utter meaningless words and numbers. This, approximately, is what denizens of Las Vegas casinos do all the time. Come to think, maybe Las Vegas is a Fellini film. Perhaps one day he will dub in dialogue:

Chalky-faced woman with an obviously atrophied and barely functioning emotional apparatus rhythmically and interminably inserts coins into and jerks down handle of vividly colored brilliantly functional slot machine. Clickety-click, it whirs, and clinkety-clink, it spews a glittering splash of coins into its smooth pelvic dish.

WOMAN: *You love me.*
SLOT MACHINE: *I am you.*

Gradually, images of slot machine and woman merge, its vivid functioning entity displacing her pale and wasted interior, and she plays on as the machine melds with her until it is within her, inside.

It is all inside, the real stuff of the act of gambling, whether the gambler is in Freeport or San Juan, Santa Anita or on the phone with a bookie. It is inside. Psychiatry agrees at least on that, and I personally lean hard on an axiom that has ever saved me from utter bafflement at mankind. Behavior may be irrational, but it still serves a purpose.

On its face, the gambler's game is irrational. So, shrink-like, I took for granted it could be understood only as a dramatization, a rite serving some emotional purpose. Somewhere, however, I departed from other theorists on the purpose it might serve. It seemed to me they assumed too much. Knowing that the gambler inevitably loses, they assumed that this—the loss—served his unconscious need. Hence suspicions of masochism or self-punishment for the guilt-ridden.

I eventually saw it a different way. My gamblers seemed to get their special feeling, the compelling thing, not at the resolution of a bet, not at the winning or losing, but while the bet was pending. While the gamble was pending resolution they knew those special sensations, almost indescribable. The feelings vanish when the gamble is resolved, but they want them again, and so they bet again, and again. Inevitably they lose, because the system is rigged that way; but as I came to hear them, betting itself brings that intense experience—an enigmatically ambiguous one. It begins when the betting begins. My hope was to locate the emotional purpose this might serve. The task took a lot of listening.

I sat listening to David K., 37, a bachelor, in one of those musky-dusky Manhattan saloons. It was a Third Avenue place where the men shift about like wisps of smog, and you wonder whether the bedrheumy ladies yearn to bump into a coprophemiac. Naturally, no one seemed startled when David loudly spoke of his sex life. He was a thick carrot of a man, stocky, with a striped lavender shirt, dark hair, questing eyes, a predatory presence, and he spoke with uncommon candor.

"The value of life to me is titillation and excitement," he said. "I need blatant pleasures, instant titillation." Without this, life was "a void," and gambling filled this void—as, in high school, football had sometimes filled it, certain tense and uncertain moments he had known playing defensive guard. He had yearned to play the professional game, a dream relinquished when he failed to make his varsity team in college, "In a way," he said, "I've spent my life on the two-yard line."

Betting on sports became his thing. When winning, David would "live like a king." Each week he would feel special feelings. "It appealed to my brinker instinct, the feeling of teetering on the brink. When you are gambling, the juices are flowing, you are *really* alive, *really* alive."

A circle of swinging friends made his penthouse their scene. Yet David, while gambling, felt peculiarly alone. "When gambling, I lose all feeling for other people," he said. In any event, his life included but one other interest that he acknowledged. "I love sex," he proclaimed loudly, "I really love sex. But, you know, gambling even spoils sex. You tune in WHN, and they give scores every quarter hour or so, and so while you are making it you begin to listen for this and, you know, all of a sudden you are *somewhere else*."

In bad times, David was sustained by a lucrative family owned insurance company. Such a time had arrived at the moment we talked. He had lost disastrously, so had moved out of his penthouse. He was working as an executive in the family firm, and bored with it, still trying to find a way to displace the gambling hunger. He excused himself when it came time for him to join his square younger brother and take their mother to the Waldorf for her customary birthday dinner. Three hours this articulate man spent generously telling me of every phase of his personal life. He never mentioned his father.

I pondered this, and listened on, and several gamblers later, I pondered still. "You'll never find a common denominator," one card addict warned me, meaning I would find no single common cause for the gambler's appetite. Well, I wasn't quite looking for a single common cause. I was look-

51

ing for common traits, common sensations in the gambler's life, common tendencies, habits, turns of mind.

These emerged. Gamblers commonly indulged the grandiose self-projection, wistfully yearning for the king's life, or Riley's. Personal insularity was common, an inability to feel for others, a cloistered inner life, a tendency to loveless sex, using women, without emotional engagement, as masturbational instruments. Gamblers were commonly known for their lying—and most admitted it. It was simply another way of guarding their secret inner world. They guarded it while betting, with that numb visage known as the poker face, though it is scarcely limited to the poker table. They commonly felt special power, and some voice beyond them would tell them they would win.

Most important to me, however, was the universality of the central gambling experience—that feeling of which David K. spoke, the sensation of being "really alive." Over and again I heard the identical phrase, or the same idea. Some gamblers leaped to different words to express it. Eventually, however, I saw that something extraordinary is induced by gambling. The gambling gambler enters a special state of being. Hard put to define it, he may say as did David that the "juices are flowing" or that he feels "a high, a high" with his "heart pounding" and "something electrical happening in there." It is not merely elation, not merely pleasurable, not simply like feeling good as contrasted with feeling bad. It is strange and "tingling" within him, secret and intricate and curiously taut, thrumming with tensions that evade words. Even so, the essence of the experience stands clear—from the gambler's own language. This thing brings the gambler assurance that he exists. When his insides are full of this feeling, this amalgam of conflicting and inseparable emotions, he knows that this is how life is.

I couldn't learn this without learning the obverse. Away from gambling, the gambler's state of being grows dim, wan, tenuous, doubtful, uncomfortable. Life seems "a void." He feels "restless," "anxious," and "something is wrong." He feels "bored, bored, bored," and is "jittery, in a hurry to get going." If he can't bet, he may become "physically sick." He does not, in short, feel like himself—until he bets.

I marvel that gambling can erase such symptoms. Yet it does—not when the gambler has won or lost but when he gets his bet down. Then, to use that odd slang word, he is in "action." "Action" he can obtain slouched in bed, phone at the ear. "Action" he can get hunched over a kidney-shaped blackjack table, immobile, signaling hits with the flick of a finger. Action. Supposedly the word speaks to the process of betting. I suspect it speaks more deeply to what happens within the gambler. He places the bet, the juices flow, he feels really alive: *action*. When the bet is on, his existence is confirmed.

Knowing this, I wondered no longer why the gambler gambled. Nothing is more important to any man than the thing that confirms his existence, his sense of himself. I stood now at another question or two: What had given the gambler such a peculiar sense of himself? And how did gambling confirm it? It was deep within, somewhere, and in gambling, he re-experienced it. I had to look for the way in which the gambler had come to know what it is to be alive—and had found it to be this strange thing of profoundly conflicting emotions.

I had to peer deep, so I listened, surprised no longer that the gambler's game proved so intense, that it filled him up with this special thing, packing him full, driving out all else, love filial, love sexual, love marital. "On our honeymoon, I got on the phone and started betting, and that was the end of the honeymoon," said one. And another: "There was no sex between me and my wife the last year and a half that I gambled." To those of us reared on Freudian dogma, it should tell something of the power of this thing. Another

53

gambler speaks: "The family felt that what I had done with the money killed my father, so they wouldn't let me come to the funeral, wouldn't let me in the church, so I turned tail and headed for the track." And a Miami gambler's wife: "There was a prowler outside, and I was terrified, and so I called him at the hotel where he was playing gin, and he said he would come right home—after the game."

Suckers, they call them, and I mulled this word. I became so diagnostic by Los Angeles that when a writer told me of renting a gambler's girl friend for $250 to join a mate-swapping club with him, I couldn't enjoy the kicker of his story. While the writer cackled toward my vichyssoise, I took note that the gambler had the kind of girl who could be rented. Suckers—the word reeked of infantile charades. And some feeling of omnipotence was another common trait, one that plagues many of us, the feeling of mysterious power that lingers with us from the days of infancy, those days when a squawk of rage would fill our hungry mouths with a nipple. We were all little suckers once.

I had to look toward childhood, because that's where it happens, that's where you find out what life is really like. So I went on listening, harvesting tatters of memory, marveling at man's peculiar willingness to tell the truth once he is assured no one will ever know he did it. I was pledged to lie about their names, so they talked openly, most of them, talked in saloons, offices, apartments, the Jai alai *frontón* in Miami. Listen:

"I was basically a loner." Here's Charlie, 39, salesman, avid gambler at cards in college, later on dice, sports, anything. "Reading the results, I could not have cared less. I just wanted to bet. The experience I was trying to get was excitement, danger. I was trying to get as close to the edge of the cliff as possible. I had a sense of fearlessness..."

(Charlie and I met in a New York building at a moment when it was being evacuated because of a bomb threat. He thought it was all right to ignore the threat, so we sat down and talked.)

"I was really a dry well of emotion," Charlie said. "I could not cry as a kid. My parents would spank me, and I would not cry. I told my mother there is no use spanking me, you'll only hurt your hand. I didn't really have emotions. My father was a salesman, and I would very seldom see or be with him. My mother would say, 'Wait until your father gets home and he'll punish you.' My mother was an asthmatic and very sick, and I was left to take care of my sister. I went to college hoping to become an engineer, but I spent all my time gambling. My relationship with girls was completely strange. I looked for a wife who could help me stop gambling, but marriage just made me more secretive about it. After college, I went into business with my father. I was always trying to jam it to my father. The first bum check I wrote was on him. Once, I stopped gambling for a whole year. I was on edge the whole year, feeling like a dentist was drilling on me without novocaine. I didn't care about money. It was a means to achieve an end, and the end was gambling. When I was gambling, I was like a hazelnut, soft on the inside and hard on the outside. I didn't talk to anybody and let nobody talk to me."

"I never liked to hear the final score." Here's Pete, 29, who gambled himself roughly $25,000 into debt by April, 1969. "A seventh-inning score, I could listen to that, but the final score would just ruin me. With a bet on a game, your whole body is involved in that game. At the end, there was no excitement. I was dead inside. When I lost, I would put everything aside for a half hour. I would just lie down. Then I'd start to wheel and deal—where to get the money? If I could not bet that night, I was physically sick. I would bet all the major-league games, and then I'd make the bookie give me some action on the minor leagues. I dropped a thousand like it was nothing. I would lie just to make people think I had a winner. I could tell lies so well that I believed them. I liked playing the big shot, picking up all the checks. I was in a world of isolation, and it was one of the worst things that ever happened to me. I was in a shell. I was afraid to face people. We'd have guests, and I'd be off in another room, leaving them to talk to my wife. I created fights just to get out of the house. I never had compassion. Compassion for what! Who ever had compassion for me! I could have signed a contract to play pro baseball. My father had died, and my mother did not want me to leave home. I had to work, so I didn't sign."

"Well, my father died when I was about 18 months old." Here's Sid, 43, and that is the first thing he utters when I invite him to tell me about his life. He sits across from me in a blue suit, his high forehead creased, his hazel eyes chasing memories around the room. "I'm the kind who would bet on anything. Where the action was, I was. Horses. Sports. After high school, I went to work as a salesman in the garment center, but I would have to be every day at the track. I got married and went to Bermuda for my honeymoon, but on the third day, the horse I had bet on in the Kentucky Derby lost, and I was on the phone betting every day, and the honeymoon was over. I was always wound up, but I had very little emotion. The emotion was always before the event. It was not the money. Sometimes I thought to myself I was going to be a millionaire, but I just thought the money would give me some kind of power, that it would make me as much as other people. I was one who did not show emotion. I always kept up a big front, I always gave the impression that everything was beautiful. I always had to be bigger than the next person because I always felt smaller than somebody else. I was closed in. When we had visitors, my wife and the others would talk, I would switch on some sports event I had bet on. When I had a bet and had money I could not sleep. I only slept good when I had no money. When I was broke, I slept like a baby."

"When I gambled, nothing else mattered. It just came first." Here's Barnie, 44, a stockroom foreman. He has told of estrangement from his family. Now he speaks of things he was uttering while making 15 straight passes with the dice in a Bleeker Street loft. "You get so hoarse. Things are coming out of your head that are crazy, really crazy. You are talking to yourself or to the dice, or you think you are talking around the room, Come 7, Come 7 . . . I guess it's like praying."

Into my own memory I gathered them, these ghosts and twinges and hungers and sadnesses and fears that were the real memories of others, and this vast accumulation moiled into an aggregate and became mine, my memory. And in its sorrowful shadows I sensed a lost child and felt that I could see—could *remember*—how he came to know what it meant to be alive.

It came to him, as to others, in one of those tenuous years of life, at seven or eight or nine, that critical moment when a life discovers its being and its flavor. The lucky ones find their being confirmed in the mirror of love, but he—this aggregate child—found himself severed from love, or imagined it to the point of knowing, knew it from a father's absence, or in parental whippings, or in parental sickness that walled him off in fathomless ways. Or he read it—the severance of love—in subtly rejecting words that would cause him to wipe his father from his memory and speak of his life as though it were fatherless.

So the truth of being alive, to him, was both to love and feel worthy of love, and to feel worthless in the face of severed love. He yearned so profoundly for the return of love that he *knew* it would return, while, simultaneously, bitter anger at the loss, anger deep beyond his knowledge, made him *know* that it was lost forever. His psyche, protecting him from sharp anguish, turned it to exquisite bittersweet self-pity;

and so powerful was his yearning, so deep his communion with it, he could hear it sometimes as a voice from beyond.

Grandiose fantasies saved him from feeling worthless: He would be a football hero, a millionaire. He could not bear the thought of another rejection: He isolated himself, lived in a shell, became a loner. He did not want to reveal love even by crying when they whipped him.

Such was the very stuff of his life: profound yearning inseparably joined with the anguish of betrayal, a thrumming tension that ran so deep and stayed so long he did not feel like himself without it. It was him, and he needed to be himself, needed—as every being needs—to reconfirm his existence over and again.

There were ways and compulsive ways to do this, but he discovered gambling, and he found that when the bets were on he suddenly felt like himself. He felt *really* alive, and inevitably so, for he had returned again to the moment when life had spoken its truth to him, when the mirror of love grew dark, when anguish in tandem with yearning became the stamp of his confirmation on earth. In action, he was living, lost child alive, running, ever running behind horses, clinging to the tingling reins, two wild horses, one Yes and one No, one Win and one Lose, one Love and one Loveless, running on, running on . . .

Some gamblers, a few, cut loose, let go, and when they do, they think—as the man was saying up there while the hard rain splattered down on Manhattan's fresh spring grime—of the love they lost and the love they were unable to find and the love they were unable to give.

And so should we all. It would help, I'll bet.

—*LOOK*, May 19, 1970

WHY THERE IS NO PLACE LIKE IT

1982

"There's no place like home for the holidays..." That certain time of year being at hand, this sentiment from *Home for the Holidays* will soon be crooning forth repetitiously from all the mellow music stations. More power to it. Only a sorehead would fuss about too much celebration of the idea of home during the festive winter season. For that matter, home deserves a good deal of hymning all the time. There is, as the wonderful old song *Home, Sweet Home* established once and for all, no place like it—and this no matter what sort of place home turns out to be. What also needs to be remembered is that home, although a special place, is never merely a place.

It is a reality that is routinely forgotten when people try to figure out the best places to live. That game goes on continually. In the 1970s the Midwest Research Institute of Kansas City put Portland, Oregon, and Sacramento at the top of the heap, after a "quality of life" survey of 243 U.S. metropolitan areas, and Birmingham and Jersey City at the bottom. This year a book called *Places Rated Almanac* scored the "livability" of 277 U.S. urban areas; it nominated Atlanta and Washington and its environs as most livable, with two Massachusetts areas—Fitchburg-Leominster and Lawrence-Haverhill—bringing up the rear. More recently, University of Pennsylvania Professor of Social Work Richard Estes turned up with an index to the "quality of life" in 107 nations. Top marks went to Denmark and Norway and booby prizes to Ethiopia and Chad (the U.S. ranked 41st, two notches above the U.S.S.R.). Surveys of this sort usually fuel chauvinistic arguments among civic booster types. But the question is: What do such studies have to do with the way people actually wind up in whatever homes they wind up with?

The answer is: little if anything. The analysts who evaluate and rank places lean entirely on objective criteria that play a relatively small role among the influences that determine where people make their homes. For one thing, the big majority of the world's people are born into the places that remain their homes for life. In the U.S., almost 64% of the people live today in the states in which they were born. It is safe to assume that few of those made a prenatal choice of birthplace on the basis of economic, political, social and cultural factors such as those used in *Places Rated Almanac*. For another, when people as adults uproot from one home to make another elsewhere, they are most often impelled by an event like a new job, almost never by the sheer allure of some other place. Given such realities, the ranking of cities and countries is bound to seem an entirely academic exercise. For people at home, the exaltation of any Elsewhere, even with hard facts, never quite makes sense. Hard facts, by definition, can never include the one fact that makes a place especially dear: the fact that it is home.

Reason alone can never fully explain the workings of the human sense of home. Down in its mystical essence, the very idea of home resists definition. While a place of nativity usually becomes home, there are those who find a home only by leaving that place for some other where they feel ineffably they belong. The notion of home becomes strangely wedded to the idea of fate. Home may be, as Pliny is supposed to have said, where the heart is, but it can also be where hate is. Human attachments to places, as to persons, are sealed by rage as well as by love. Home is clearly among the greatest values on the human scale. Cain, condemned for murdering Abel to that deprivation of home known as banishment, said: "My punishment is greater than I can bear."

The powers of home, in its play on human behavior are protean, magnetic, chimerical, profound.

The pull of home surpasses logic all the time. It keeps people living in conditions that seem (to an outsider) most improbable. It keeps people living more or less happily in deserts, in igloos, in the shadows of volcanoes and the paths of recurring floods. It has induced generations to take the winters of New Hampshire and the summers of Alabama. More, a sense of home will cause people to endure situations that an outsider free to flee, would not tolerate for a moment—political turmoil, for example, which a good deal of South America's people suffer continually. The sense of home even makes people want to return to the hateful conditions that cast them out. Author Ariel Dorfman, one of thousands of Chileans banished by the government of General Augusto Pinochet, publicly protested this month about the "intolerable homelessness" he has suffered for nine years and begged the Pinochet government: "Let us come home." "Home," said Robert Frost, "is the place where, when you have to go there, they have to let you in." But that, as the spectacle of modern politics proves, is not invariably so.

Such is the utterly subjective nature of home that the very word must fetch up a distinct and unique image and sensibility in every person. And indeed home can be many things: a house, a town, a neighborhood, a state, a country, a room. Home can be wherever one feels at home, and even a scrap of a place can mobilize that homey feeling. The old standard *Autumn in New York* plausibly evokes a person looking down on the metropolis from the 27th floor of a hotel to find that the "glittering crowds and shimmering clouds in canyons of steel—they're making me feel I'm home." Plausible? In London, Thornton Wilder once provoked astonishment by referring to his temporary accommodations as home. How use the hallowed word to refer to a hotel room? Explained Wilder: "A home is not an edifice, but an interior and transportable adjustment." It is surely that, along with all else, as immigrants to the U.S. prove over and again: while they have always embraced their adopted land as home, they have tended to ward off melting into the new place by recreating elements of the homes left behind. Result: ethnic neighborhoods as well as poignant sentiments like that of the Hungarian immigrant song recorded by Michael Kraus in *Immigration, the American Mosaic:* "We yearn to return to our little village/ Where every blade of grass understood Hungarian." Home, it seems, can also be divided, which is probably essential for a species whose fundamental dilemma can be described as simultaneous needs for mobility and a sense of home. For nomadic herdsmen, an endless path becomes—home.

Be it ever so ambiguous, there is no idea like home. Not the least of home's specialness is the fact that it can often be seen most clearly from afar. Thus it was a sojourn in Italy that inspired Robert Browning's famous "Oh, to be in England . . ." By chance, while in Paris early in the 19th century, the American Actor-Author John Howard Payne experienced some of the yearnings for home that found their way into his classic *Home, Sweet Home.* Together, Payne's song and Browning's poetry suggest that the part of home that is not merely a place exists, so to speak, in the I of the beholder. It is not quite true that you can't go home again. The deeper truth is that you never leave the part of home that becomes the movable feast of the imagination.

—*TIME*, November 29, 1982

GET THIS SEASON OFF THE COUCH!

1978

They begin turning up this time of year as reliably as gaudy lights and the Salvation Army, and with furrowed brows they hand the public a unique gift—clear warnings about the morbid hazards that lurk in the traditional seasonal celebrations. They are the jolly diagnosticians, and they dirge forth chanting their own anthem, a sort of Fugue for Handwringers, the gist of which is that there may be poisoned plums in the pudding.

The holidays, they say, and especially Christmas, inflame neurosis, trigger depression, accentuate loneliness. The very expectation of joy becomes a source of gloom. Adults get pressured into the hypocrisy of mingling with people they do not like and going to churches they do not believe in. Children get confused by the Santa hokum; they wind up either addicted to greed by too many presents or ridden with envy by too few. Families obliged to reassemble are rent by old grudges set to festering again. Furthermore, since Christmas dominates the marathon Thanksgiving-to-New Year's celebrations, non-Christians get painful left-out feelings.

This grim picture of the winter holidays accumulated in psychological literature and passed, during the last generation, into the popular domain. These days it can be casually overheard around almost any office, street corner or watering hole. Indeed, many Americans have begun to sound, and a few to act as though the appropriate way to navigate the holidays is with a clipboard and psychiatric checklist for keeping track of casualties.

So fretful is the atmosphere achieved by the clinical view that some people are even turning to ever increasing preholiday workshops that offer to help them "cope" with seasonal stress. This trend in popular therapy reached a bizarre pinnacle this year with the scheduling, in New York, of an eleven-day "antiholiday" workshop starting three days before Christmas. It was conceived by a therapist who says she and her followers hope to "create new rituals and celebrations" while at the same time they cure themselves of the old.

Admittedly, some of the pathological grist is not just humbug. The shrinks do gear up as though for combat duty during the holidays. Emotional turmoil is easily noticeable and evidently widespread. One pioneering study of Christmas neurosis, published by the University of Utah School of Medicine in the 1950s (and mined ever since by writers assigned to recycle the annual piece on "the holiday blues"), established that as many as nine out of ten people suffer "adverse emotional reactions to Christmas pressures."

The dreary litany seems endless. Even suicide is said to increase during the season, but this claim is disputed. No matter. Even if suicides decline, the rest of the diagnosis is enough to make the holiday seem like a prolonged calamity. Before Americans completely succumb to such an impression, now is the time to diagnose the diagnosis.

One need not quibble with particular findings to detect their limits. Let the stunning statistic from the Utah study stand—but add to it the universal knowledge that roughly ten out of ten people suffer "adverse emotional reactions" to life itself. Those who do not ought to have their heads examined. Even saints—especially saints—anguish. Evidently humankind from ages immemorial has known a rough time in that darkest gully of the year—the season of the winter solstice. In fact, most historians agree that it was precisely to relieve the morbidity inherent in the season that the species invented the extravagant celebrations that have endured to this day.

The old pagan celebrations, which had gone on for millenniums, continued for centuries after the birth of Christ. It was to steer the energies of the celebrants into more pious channels—so says Francis X. Weiser, S.J., in *The Christmas Book*—that the church in the 4th century picked, as Christmas Day, exactly the date that signaled the end of the Roman Saturnalia. The origin of the celebrations at least raises the question of which came first, seasonal malaise or the celebrations? Could it be that the rituals cure far more gloom than they precipitate? Surely such issues should not be abdicated entirely to social pathologists.

The trouble with the now pervasive clinical view of the holidays is that, along with offering undeserved comfort to unreconstructed Scrooges, it tends to confuse many perfectly healthy people about their own emotional condition. Even casual observation confirms that many weave through the holidays feeling vaguely like victims—acutely aware of the supposedly malignant pressures that the diagnosticians always talk about. No mystery here. With a consciousness razed by standard holiday pathology, even an intelligent adult may tend to construe the pressure as a symptom of something bad and imminent. In fact, that pressure is primarily only the moving power of a vast communal celebration. This coercive atmosphere is not just an incidental effect of the season, as some suggest, but its very essence.

Every human ritual, after all, owns the ulterior intent of pressing people out of habituated everyday behavior. Just as a parade or fiesta is intended to tug people en masse onto the streets to see and celebrate who they are, so the rites of the winter holidays are aimed at prying people out of their diurnal ruts into unaccustomed minglings, new communions, fresh gestures. The purpose of it all, undeclared and unsentimental, is to arouse a general reaffirmation of the commonality of life as the year's shortest day comes and goes. While emotionally fragile individuals may suffer special aggravations as a result, the temperamental thrash that most people feel is often no deeper than their resistance to being nudged out of narrow everyday patterns. The pressure of the season is only the mute wish of a society that yearns, against all odds, for a sense of wholeness.

But that is not a charade in psychodrama. It is the troubled world for real, and the jargon of the clinic does not begin to describe its complexities. Neither does the carping of the cynic. It is not all hypocritical to surrender to the pressure to join somehow in the celebration. It is merely human, and quite possibly of value. Even a trivial card sent by rote can sustain a tie that would otherwise vanish. A hand extended in feigned cordiality to an old adversary may turn out to have more moral worth than the embrace of an old friend. Obligatory attendance at socials, like reunions with chilly kinsmen, offers as much chance of warmth as of friction. A person even tempted to become a once-a-year churchgoer may thereby be moved to the only reflection since last year on the inscrutable powers that play over creation. Joining in, as even the professional diagnosticians insist, is the best remedy for the holiday blues.

—*TIME*, December 11, 1978

TWO

The Scientific Pursuit Of Happiness

Little Crimes Against "Nature"

Getting Dizzy By The Numbers

The Secret Life Of The Common Cold

The Weather:
Everyone's Favorite Topic

The Great American Cooling Machine

A New Distrust Of The Experts

Living Happily Against The Odds

The Scientific Pursuit Of Happiness

1979

mc^2 may well = E in the known physical universe. Nothing quite that pat can be said about the cosmos of the human temperament. In the play of emotion, logic is seldom evident, and the laws of gravity and thermodynamics never. What goes up in the psyche sometimes does not come down; the boiling points of individuals and collectives alike are impossible to fix. In light of this, it is no wonder that science long shied away from studying, or attempting to explain, that most subtle and elusive of all human moods: happiness. Instead, it happily left the field to philosophers, preachers, poets—and the swarms of author-therapists who yearly vie for bestsellerdom with new formulas for attaining this desired estate.

Lately, however, science has begun to nose around in that shifty terrain it so long neglected. Tenuous scientific probes of the happiness phenomenon, as an aspect of mental health, were organized as long ago as the 1960s. Perhaps because happiness itself was all but out of style in the days of Viet Nam, urban riots and the burgeoning dope culture, the trend never took off. Only now is it becoming clear that our gladness is likely to be subjected to the same methodical research and analysis that has been lavished for generations on our madness. The signs that happyology is aborning as a discipline have come in sequences of earnest surveys, widespread drizzles of articles and now a spate of hardback tomes.

An archetype of the current genre is *Happy People*, by Columbia Psychology Professor Jonathan Freedman. It promises to reveal "what happiness is, who has it and why."

Freedman analyzes the results of both popular surveys and casual interviews and also attempts, he says, "to present what we, as social scientists, know about happiness." Soon to be published is *Optimism: The Biology of Hope*, by Rutgers University Anthropologist Lionel Tiger; it explores the possible biological origins of the human sanguineness that underlies feelings of well-being, whatever they are called. New York Psychoanalyst Willard Gaylin has just weighed in with a study called *Feelings: Our Vital Signs*, which scrutinizes and tries to delineate all the familiar varieties of human feeling. Gaylin thus probes the character of a state that he calls not "happiness" but "feeling good."

A proliferation of less ambitious studies and surveys, some of them amounting to market research, has occurred in the past few years. The University of Michigan Institute for Social Research conducted a nationwide study of income and education as determinants of happiness. The advertising firm Batten, Barton, Durstine and Osborn carried out a similar but broader survey to find out whether their clients' potential consumers "were happier . . . than other segments of the population." Scientific studies of worker "contentment" have been going on for years, to be sure, but are not quite the same as the new wave of investigations into the larger character of well-being. It may be too soon to say where these new excursions will lead, but it is not too early to inquire.

First off, analytical scrutiny of happiness should not be confused with preaching about it. Books hustling formulas and drills are supposed to produce happiness circulate these days in numbers that are too great to count, let alone mention. These products of the booming feel-good industry invariably try to evoke happiness, but they seldom describe or analyze it. That, of course, is the fascination of the scientific challenge. The feel-good trade's blizzard of lighter-than-air tracts proves nothing whatever about happiness except that a lot of people are willing to pay for help in pursuing it.

The new happyologists are doing a bit better than that, though their young science is now approximately where navigation was before the invention of the compass. In some ways, as Humorist Russell Baker recently observed, the happyologists resemble sociologists in their dedication to proving what everybody has known all along. Baker groaned at the supposedly big discovery that an unhappy childhood does not necessarily lead to an unhappy adulthood. Who could fail to echo his groan when it is reported, as though it were news, that money, beyond some uncertain minimum, does not buy happiness? A horselaugh might even be the appropriate response when Psychoanalyst Gaylin declares: "It is . . . good to 'feel good.'"

The one thing common to most of the research is the conspicuous wariness of the investigators. The utterly elusive ingredients of the mood they are examining force them to turn away from the phenomenon itself. They prefer to tabulate its incidence and parameters. So, even though they maintain their scientific detachment and method in analyzing data, to collect it they have had no convenient choice but to adopt the time-tested techniques of public opinion polling. Subjects are asked merely to declare their degree of happiness, not define it. Even Pollster Louis Harris turns up as an unlikely temporary happyologist, reporting for this month's *Playboy* that while 49% of American men rank sexual satisfaction as "very important" to happiness, 84% give that same crucial weight to family life.

Not all the early discoveries are that breathtaking, although many of them come in similar statistical form. Findings may vary from survey to survey, but seldom astonishingly. Some results that fail to amaze can still be heartening. Most studies so far confirm that happiness does not depend on any single factor. That is, neither geographical location nor financial status nor age is a determinant of happiness. The happy are slightly more likely to be married, but unhappiness is anything but epidemic among the single. Neither the young, the middle-aged nor the old have any special claim on happiness.

People who like their jobs (and up to 82% claim to) tend to be happier in general. An attitude of optimism (held by some 70%) often coincides with happiness, but quite a few of the 6% who are convinced pessimists are also happy. Good health is a big factor in happiness to some, yet poor health does not turn out to be incompatible with happiness. Not even "satisfaction" is indispensable to happiness. Says University of Michigan Psychologist Stephen Withey in *Subjective Elements of Well-Being*, a collection of papers presented in 1972: "Young people tend to report more happiness than satisfaction, while older people tend to say that they are more satisfied than they are happy."

The incongruous and even adverse situations that seem to support happiness may only confirm the insight ventured by turn-of-the-century Psychologist William James. "Life and its negation," wrote James, "are beaten up inextricably together. The two are equally essential facts of existence and all natural happiness thus seems infected with a contradiction." One broad contradiction that emerges from the happiness surveys is that, in spite of all the reports of the emptiness of modern life, relatively few people consider themselves very unhappy. On the contrary, an overwhelming majority of Americans (60% in one survey, 70% in another, 86% in a third) consider themselves reasonably happy. Only the heartless could be harsh toward the science that bears such tidings.

Still, happyology has defaulted so far on the really big question: Why are people happy or why not? And more fundamental, what is happiness? The young science is far from the practical goal of providing guidance on how to attain happiness. "Alas," says Freedman, "the overwhelming finding of all the research is that there is no easy solution, no foolproof strategy for finding it."

Lionel Tiger's forthcoming book offers some slightly more definite advice—or at least postulation. Although he is not studying happiness as such, the anthropologist argues that humankind does not have to go looking far for its basic source of well-being: it is built right into the human body. Says he: "Our benign sense of the future could have been bred into us and other complex animals out of the need to survive." Tiger speculates that man pushes ever onward, inextinguishably optimistic in the face of adversity, because of his biochemistry. The key to mankind's optimism, he argues, lies in those lately discovered substances called endorphins. These are the morphine-like chemical agents that the body itself produces, sending them into special sites of the brain and spinal cord to reduce pain. In this, says Tiger, "we may be on the way to finding a specific source for notions of personal well-being. Endorphins may not serve principally to reduce pain. Their major function may be to anesthetize the organism against responding too directly and forcefully to negative cognitive stimuli in the environment. They permit the animal to obscure the understanding that its situation is dire."

If that is so, people who anesthetize themselves with booze or pot may be trying to achieve unnaturally what endorphins do naturally. Still, since individual body chemistries vary, the endorphin theory might account for the fact that some people are habitually happier than others: some might just have a bigger supply of this natural analgesic. It may even suggest, moreover, one concrete way in which human beings might assure their sense of happiness; yet this way—the ingestion of synthetic endorphins—is unnervingly like the drug-popping route to happiness envisioned in *Brave New World*. In all this, alas, nothing much is added to the question that has always nagged the brave *old* world: Just what is happiness?

Given time, the happyologists could conceivably come up with a useful, or at least a discerning, answer. Perhaps the question is so fundamental that, like love and wisdom, it will always elude human definition. For the moment, surely, it can be answered decisively, for better or worse, only by each individual. In short, the considerable resources, even good intentions, of science have so far disclosed little about happiness that was not available in the words of Seneca ("Unblest is he who thinks himself unblest") in ancient times or those of Abe Lincoln ("Most folks are about as happy as they make up their minds to be") in a more recent epoch. Happiness, in short, awaits its Newton, its Galileo.

—*TIME*, March 19, 1979

Little Crimes Against "Nature"

1982

> *Folks are dumb where I come from*
> *They ain't had any learnin'*
> *Still they're happy as can be*
> *Do-In What Comes Nat-ur-'lly*
>
> —Irving Berlin,
> *Doin' What Comes Natur'lly*

Smart Americans as well as dumb ones have always held a special belief in what comes nat-ur-'lly. That belief appears to grow stronger as society pulls further away from nature. As ever more synthetic artifacts of Western civilization emerge from laboratories and test tubes, a great many people have developed an outright crush on nature. Indeed, the supposedly natural is so warmly regarded nowadays that the artificial is in danger of getting an unjustly bad name.

There is nothing wrong with loving nature. The trouble is that in the commercial rush to exploit this popular sentiment the notion of what is natural is getting stretched absurdly out of shape. It is even possible these days to see references to colors called natural vinyl and natural nylon. Considering nature's own glaring penchant for diverse and gaudy colors, it is illogical that any anemic shade should be called (as convention calls it) natural. And it is preposterous to put that label on synthetic stuff. If man-made plastics possess a natural color, then it is fair to ask: What is the natural color of a Buick?

The results of human artifice are one thing, the effects of nature are another. A raccoon's coat is natural, a raccoon coat is not. Hair grows naturally on the human head, but its naturalness vanishes the instant it is groomed with comb, brush, scissors or curlers. The term natural, in its strictest sense, should not be applied to anything contrived or even changed by man. Some philosophers, to be sure, encourage a soupy sort of reductionism. "Nature who made the mason, made the house," wrote Ralph Waldo Emerson. That notion is nonsense. It is plain as rain that people invented the house to escape the elements of nature.

Mankind would never have got anywhere without outwitting or overpowering the natural order of things. Early humans invented the arts of agriculture and livestock management to free themselves from dependency on the uncertain bounty of nature. Crucial differences between things devised by humankind and those that issue from Mother Nature often get blurred in the cause of merchandising.

An amazing variety of goods goes to market these days identified either directly or by insinuation as natural, or as nature's, or as conducive to naturalness. Bloomingdale's, that barometer of with-itness, features jeans made of "natural stonewashed denim." Golden Key Creations of Fort Worth urges customers; "Be pure, natural, beautiful with Vitamin E cream!" Breeder's Choice Pet Foods has launched a new line of "all natural" dog food, which is the regular line bereft of additives, and Weleda, Inc., of Spring Valley, New York, sells "an all-natural, non-aerosol spray deodorant." Bootstrap Press of Glendale, California, offers a book that teaches "the deep natural breathing you were born with."

The national boom in fresh-from-the-factory natural foods shows no signs of abating. There is hardly a department of any supermarket that does not offer some sort of comestible with "nature" or "natural" on the label. Hershey's Semi-Sweet Chocolate Chips boasts "all natural ingredients." Snyder's of Hanover pretzels are said to be natural, as though just plucked off the old pretzel tree. Mrs. Paul's French Fried

Onion Rings? "Only from natural fresh sliced onions." Ice cream may be a man-made culinary artifact, but here comes Schrafft's Light "all natural ice milk." Beer making may entail an intricate legacy of culture and chemistry, but there goes Anheuser-Busch Natural Light beer. Arnold's now puts out a Nature-l bread, Kraft's a natural cheddar cheese, Heinz a natural vinegar. Mrs. Smith's Bake and Serve Pie may contain artificial color and flavor, monoglycerides, diglycerides and the antioxidant BHA, but it also includes, or so the label says, "natural juice" apple. The phrase inevitably provokes a question: Where to find any perfectly natural commercial fruit? The answer, of course, is that almost all agricultural products since the heyday of Luther Burbank are hybrids that were developed or improved by state agricultural departments. An apple today is not necessarily natural just because man has not yet made it square—like the tomato.

These promiscuous claims of naturalness have become something of an embarrassment to people who are supposed to know what they mean. Says Jules Rose, board chairman of Sloan's Supermarkets: "The term natural foods drives me crazy because no one has come up with the right definition." The Federal Trade Commission's Consumer Protection Bureau has more or less evaded the issue by relying on a definition of naturalness that boils down to "minimally processed"—that is, food unchanged except by cutting, grinding, drying or pulping. This elastic notion may be comfortable for merchandisers but cannot possibly help preserve a clear sense of what is natural.

Nowhere does the idea take a more gratuitous bruising than in the field of cosmetics. Ever since the 1960s, when hostility to technology began turning the so-called natural look into a hot advertising gambit, the cosmetics industry has been overworking its overripe imagination to convince customers that naturalness is to be had only through the use of ointments, lotions, tints and other exotic stuffs. Gillette's "new FOHO—For Oily Hair Only—system" all but ineluctably boasts "natural ingredients." Jojoba oil is plugged as "nature's own deep moisturizing formula from the legendary desert plant." The epitome of the natural cosmetics notion must be a product called Natural Image by Granny's Girl: "all-natural, grown-up cosmetics especially for little girls! Blushers, Lip Glosses and Eyeshadows that give gentle hints of color, shine and scent . . ." What is easily forgotten under the enchantment of such copy is the unadorned fact that cosmetics exist entirely as interventions against natural appearances.

Finally, civilization itself is humanity's definitive intervention against what is truly natural. No matter how wrong Jean Jacques Rousseau was about the nobility of the natural savage, he correctly saw that social order "does not come from nature." Neither does much of what goes into society's consumer goods. Far too often, as Physicians Stephen Barrett and Victor Herbert write in *Vitamins & "Health" Foods: The Great American Hustle*, the natural label is nothing but "a magic sales gimmick." The resulting confusion may not be a mortal danger, but it is hardly innocent. Unchecked, it is bound to make it harder for rising generations to maintain a clear notion of the truly natural to which mankind indeed remains tied. Not long ago, a Chiffon margarine commercial got a lot of mileage out of the line "It's not nice to fool Mother Nature." It is even less nice to blame and credit her for things beyond her doing.

—*TIME*, October 11, 1982

Getting Dizzy By The Numbers

1979

"The very hairs of your head," says *Matthew 10: 30*, "are all numbered." There is little reason to doubt it. Increasingly, everything tends to get numbered one way or another, everything that can be counted, measured, averaged, estimated or quantified. Intelligence is gauged by a quotient, the humidity by a ratio, the pollen by its count, and the trends of birth, death, marriage and divorce by rates. In this epoch of runaway demographics, society is as often described and analyzed with statistics as with words. Politics seems more and more a game played with percentages turned up by pollsters, and economics a learned babble of ciphers and indexes that few people can translate and apparently nobody can control. Modern civilization, in sum, has begun to resemble an interminable arithmetic class in which, as Carl Sandburg put it, "numbers fly like pigeons in and out of your head."

Most of this numbering is useful, and a good deal of it is indispensable. In any event, the world could hardly have wound up otherwise. Human beings began counting and "falling under the spell of numbers," in H.G. Wells' words, well before they could write. Long ago, the entire species was like some modern aboriginal peoples (the Damara and some Hottentots in Africa, for example) who possess words only for numbers up to three, every larger quantity being simply expressed as "many." A fascination with the multiplicity of things, together with a quenchless scientific yen, pushed the main body of mankind, however, inevitably into its present plight—a time when so many stunning measurements are bandied about that numbers plunge in and out of the brain more like galaxies than pigeons.

The trouble is that with everything on earth (and off, too) being quantified, micro and macro, the world is becoming woefully littered with numbers that defy useful comprehension. Biology, for example, estimates that the human brain contains some 1 trillion cells. But can any imagination get a practical hold on such a quantity? It is easy to picture the symbolic numerals: 1,000,000,000,000. Still, who can comprehend that many individual units of anything at one time? The number teases, dazzles the mind and even dizzies it, but that does not add up to understanding. Biology ought to find out what happens to the brain when it tries to visualize 1 trillion.

Boggling figures of that sort have been popular as curiosities ever since Archimedes tried to calculate how many grains of sand the universe could contain (10^{51}, he said). Today, however, mind-walloping numbers are no longer oddities; they are the stuffing of ordinary news and public discourse. While even the biggest figures no doubt possess meaning, it is impossible not to suspect that many casually circulated numbers might as well be the music of the spheres.

Nowadays the commonest statistics about the world and the nation—from the megatonnages of the SALT debate to the dollars of the defense budget—tend to defeat the ordinary imagination. The world population is supposedly 4.2 billion. The nation's G.N.P. is running at about $2.39 trillion. Washington debates whether defense spending will increase to as much as $122 billion. In truth, far smaller figures can overtax ordinary people, many of whom, after all, have trouble fathoming the weather service's temperature-humidity index.

Scientific news is loaded with even more forbidding challenges. Voyager I, it seems, found a hot spot in the vicinity of Jupiter that is 300 million to 400 million degrees centigrade. Later, Voyager II, going almost 45,000 m.p.h., came as close as 404,000 miles to Jupiter's cloud tops on its way to

79

Uranus—some 1.6 billion miles out there. Science now has an electron microscope that can magnify 20 million times and so can photograph a particle with a diameter of about 4 billionths of an inch. Computers can do 80 million calculations a second (and ostensibly 6.9 trillion a day). Other recent news: a suspicion that the proton, a basic natural building block, may be unstable. It may indeed be decaying at such a rate that it would peter out in a million billion billion billion years. The effect of that notion is finally not mathematical but purely poetic.

It is not clear at just what magnitude (or diminutude) a number passes beyond the capacity of an ordinary person to grasp—that is, to picture the quantity. Yet obviously a great effort is required even to cope with what is symbolized by a billion. The proof lies in those familiar tormented illustrations that writers cook up in the hope of suggesting the amount of a billion: the 125-mile-high stack of dollar bills that would add up to about a billion, the airplane propeller turning around the clock at 2,400 r.p.m. that would fall short of spinning a billion times in a year, the fact that a billion minutes ago (A.D.77) the Christian era had scarcely got under way. Still, such efforts to evoke the actuality of a billion are far likelier to give the curious a picture of an extremely tall stack of currency than of the quantity of a billion units. In truth, most mega-numbers (and micro-numbers) that fly by these days paralyze the mind almost as much as a googol.

10,000,000,000,000,000,000,000,000,000,000,000,000,000,000,000,000,000,000,000,000,000,000,000,000,000,000,000,000,000,000,000,000,000,000,000.

Indeed, the googol might be a good symbol for a time when the world is under the sway of technology, when it has no choice, as Jacques Ellul says in *The Technological Society*, but to "don mathematical vestments." The googol is the figure 1 followed by 100 zeros (see above). It was made famous, or infamous, in the 1930s by Mathematician Edward

Kasner. He also offered the googolplex, which is 1 followed by a googol of zeros—so many zeros, said Kasner, that no matter how tiny they could not all be written on a piece of paper as wide as the visible universe.

It could be that the googol's emergence marked the time when mankind's fascination with indigestible numbers slipped beyond the pale. In the same decade that the googol appeared Sir Arthur Eddington opened his absolutely serious book, *The Philosophy of Physical Science*, with the sentence: "I believe there are 15,747,724,136,275,002,577, 605,653,961,181,555,468,044,717,914,527,116,709,366,231, 425,076,185,631,031,296 protons in the universe and the same number of electrons."

Plainly, a world that feeds on such impenetrable figures suffers a peculiar compulsion that might be called googolmania. The hunger is, whatever else, a marvel to behold, providing the spectacle of a species unable to solve a 13% inflation rate, yet eager to be informed by the *Guinness Book of World Records* that the world weighs 6,585,600,000,000,000,000,000 tons.

The human craving for numbers tells a good deal about mankind. It is both sign and cause of man's long trek from the days of one, two, three, many. It can be taken as a symptom of exuberant joy in the quantity and multiplicity of things. Still, the dizzy acceptance of those truly incomprehensible figures might also be construed as a vicarious variation of the old Faustian game: the yearning to know the unknowable.

So far, the game has not cost the species its unquantifiable soul. Enough of that remains to nurture widespread excitement over, let us say, a World Series. A googol may not tell us much about where we stand today, but even Edward Kasner would have appreciated the true human relevance of 4-3 Pirates.

—*TIME,* October 29, 1979

THE SECRET LIFE
OF THE COMMON COLD

1981

"Do you know what it is to succumb to an insurmountable day mare—a whoresome lethargy—an indisposition to do anything—a total deadness and distaste—a suspension of vitality—an indifference to locality—a numb soporifical goodfornothingness—an ossification all over—an oyster-like insensibility to the passing events—a mind stupor—a brawny defiance to the needles of a thrusting-in conscience?"

Charles Lamb groaned forth that question in the 19th century, but anybody in any epoch ought to be able to answer it with a simple yes. Anybody, that is, who has ever had a cold. Even people who have never had a cold, if any there be, are pretty likely to know something about the peculiar miseries of the ailment. After all, nobody old enough to understand talk could easily avoid all knowledge of the cold: it is one disease that has never been discussed in whispers.

Quite the contrary. People, even when hoarse, tend to discourse clearly and repetitiously about the common cold. Cold victims routinely elucidate their suffering; those who are ordinarily laconic grow voluble, and the normally gabby become windy, lugubrious. With or without colds, people eagerly pass around whatever they possess of society's huge accumulation of folklore on the subject. (Benjamin Franklin was an archetypal expert on avoiding colds: convinced that fresh air would do the job, Franklin once explained his theory so thoroughly to John Adams that he put the future President to sleep.) There are certain cold sufferers, true, who snuffle around telling everybody that the affliction is not as bad as it is cracked up to be but their stoicism does not require them to talk any less about it.

As the new cold season now arriving will demonstrate, almost nobody suffers the common cold in silence. Yet very little can usefully be said on the subject, because the common cold remains a little black hole of a disease, ultimately obscure and myth-ridden. Science, to be sure, has learned a good deal about the cold. One unsettling modern discovery is that the invisible nature of the ailment is amazingly varied. The common cold is in fact caused by 200 or so distinct viruses. Medical science, of course, has not mastered the knack of immunizing against any of them. So the state of the art of cold prevention can be boiled down to a very few words based on the discovery that colds are transmitted person to person, most often by hand. The best, still imperfect cold avoidance program thus consists of washing the hands frequently when colds are about and keeping the hands away from the nose and eyes. The state of the art of curing the cold is simpler still: there is no cure. The adage holds: with proper treatment a cold can be ended in seven days, but otherwise it lasts a week.

The paucity of verified knowledge about colds could never be deduced by anybody studying a typical cold season. Mere facts about the disease usually vanish into persisting clouds of folklore. The belief that dampness, chilliness and drafts cause colds, though debunked repeatedly in controlled experiments, is still widely held—and energetically perpetuated by parents in cautioning children. "Don't get your feet wet, you'll catch cold." Even though medical research has long since shown that neither antihistamines nor any other medication can change the course of a cold, Americans spend some $1 billion a year on untold thousands of over-the-counter cold products.

Then there are the folk remedies. These are also beyond numbering, but include traditional notables like hot toddy, hot lemonade, chicken broth, regional potions like the South's horehound and pine-needle tea, and ethnic preparations featuring ingredients like honey, garlic and cayenne. Faith is widespread in the anticold potency of herbs like eucalyptus, mullein leaves, bloodroot and red clover. California Herb Specialist Michael Tierra commends a concoction of honeysuckle, chrysanthemum and licorice.

Perhaps the most popular new folk remedy of modern times is ascorbic acid, a.k.a. vitamin C. Ever since Nobel-Prizewinning Chemist Linus Pauling popularized this remedy in the 1970 book *Vitamin C and the Common Cold,* many people have become convinced that big doses of ascorbic acid help ward off or ameliorate colds; controlled experiments, however, have failed to provide proof of the claim. Some folk remedies out of folklore (rub socks with onions, coat body with Vaseline) are hard to consider with a straight face, and a great many others irresistibly bring to mind Robert Benchley's personal anticold regimen: "Don't breathe through your nose or mouth."

It is easy to understand pre-Copernican beliefs in a flat earth and similarly easy to account for the accumulation of popular myths about the cold before the disease's viral nature became clear. But why do so many dubious beliefs persist in the face of new knowledge? The inertia of human prejudices is only part of the answer. An additional reason lies in the truth that a cold, typically, is far more than a mere medical event. Were it only that, the public would deal with the cold with far less conversation, far less drama, and the cold sufferer would never have become one of the cartoonist's regular stock of sympathetic (and pathetic) figures. The fact is that over the generations the cold has grown to be, along with all else, a theatrical event, a psychological event, a social event—all transactions that would be undermined if people laid aside myths and paid too close attention to scientific truth.

The common cold's theatricality is so obvious that one can classify the styles of cold suffering by labeling the roles that get played: the hero (who insists on coming to work), the martyr (who cannot afford not to come to work), the opportunist (who would not dream of staying away from work for less than a week). To specialists like Robert H. Waldman, chairman of the department of medicine at the West Virginia University School of Medicine, the cold as psychological event seems almost as clear. Waldman points out that the cold allows the typical adult to retreat from everyday pressures, adding: "If we did away with it—if we cured the common cold—we might well have to face an increase in hypertension, depression and related problems." Nobody who has either received or poured forth the human sympathy that a good cold provokes can fail to be convinced that one of the disease's fortunate aspects is entirely social.

Given the cost of colds, as well as the outright danger they represent when they attack somebody who is otherwise seriously ailing, the search for a way to prevent them must go on. But everybody should be forewarned that if the search ever succeeds the cold will be missed in more ways than one.

—*TIME*, November 16, 1981

The Weather: Everyone's Favorite Topic

1978

At this time of year especially, weather is on everyone's mind—and on everyone's tongue. It is Topic A everywhere, more apt to be chatted about than money, food, sex or even scandals. Nor is it regarded as trivial small talk—"the discourse of fools," as an English proverb has it. Indeed, it is fodder for the conversation of board chairman and bored charwoman, of young and old, of the bright, the dull, the rich and the poor. As if this basic coin of conversation needed to be gilded, the average American constantly reads about the weather in his newspapers and magazines, listens to regular forecasts of it on the radio and watches while some TV prophet milks it for cuteness on the evening news.

Since the weather is to man what the waters are to fish, his preoccupation with it serves a unique purpose, constituting a social phenomenon all its own. Far from arising merely to pass the time or bridge a silence, "weathertalk," as it might be called, is a sort of code by which people confirm and salute the sense of community they discover in the face of the weather's implacable influence. By dispensing a raging blizzard, a driving rainstorm or even a sunny day, the weather tends to ameliorate the estrangements inherent in cultural divisions and social stratifications. Inspired by exceptional weather, otherwise immutable strangers suddenly find themselves in communion. In the spoken code, all those weathered cliches—"Cold enough for you?" "Good day for ducks, huh?" "Gonna be a hot one!" "What a day!"—mean the same thing: "We are, after all, in this boat together."

The boat sails on, buffeted by the winds, tossed by the waters, drenched by the heavens—its inhabitants subject not only to the physical effects of the weather but to its metaphysical sway as well. People everywhere, including the U.S., confront the weather with marvelously confused feelings and attitudes. They love it as an unrivaled spectacle and fear it as an unrivaled destroyer. One day they curse the rain, the next they dream of walking in it barefooted with a lover. They study meteorology in school, while clinging to the conviction that the weather can be forecast on the basis of the behavior of bugs, animals and vegetation. Groundhog day is still observed.

As victims, people hate to cancel a picnic on account of rain, and yet they often cheer when the weather brings human activity to an abrupt standstill. Very few people are like Blaise Pascal, who insisted: "The weather and my mood have little connection." Most feel that the weather indeed affects their moods, and yet a gloomy day does not necessarily mean a gloomy disposition for all: a book before the hearth, an afternoon of tinkering in the basement or an extended visit to the local bar pleases some people as well as the brightest sun. And at least one study of test scores seemed to suggest that the occasion of a violent storm stimulated the intellectual performance of an entire class of students.

The prime oddity in the whole snarl of attitudes is the fact that almost everybody develops perverse pride in abominable weather when it happens to be their own. Abroad, there are the desert tribes that profess to revere their baked domains. Similarly, the New Englander or the Minnesotan boasts about his frozen Februarys and the snow that waits till spring before uncovering the earth again. The Deep Southerner seems proud of those stifling summers that reduce everybody to sweat and distemper. Human responses to weather are, in sum, as variable as the weather itself.

If man sees the weather differently according to his circumstance, healthy fear works at the hub of his obsession with it. Facing the awesome grandeur and cruel humors of the weather, ancient man was forced to attribute the mysterious cosmic moil to deities. Wishing desperately to better his odds against the weather (or lessen its against him), he invented innumerable prayers, supplications, sacrifice, all intended to coax the gods to bestow better weather. Wanting exactly like modern man to know about tomorrow's wind, he developed the practice of looking for omens of coming weather in the conduct of animals, the tones of the sky or the turnings of foliage. He tried rituals, such as dancing, to control the weather. They did not work, of course, but they made for some lively times.

Through human history, weather has altered the march of events and caused some mighty cataclysms. Since Columbus did not know where he was going or where he had arrived when he got there, the winds truly deserve nearly as much credit as he for the discovery of America. Ugly westerlies helped turn the 1588 Spanish Armada away from England in a limping panic. Napoleon was done in twice by weather: once by the snow and cold that forced his fearful retreat from Moscow, later by the rain that bedeviled him at Waterloo and caused Victor Hugo to write: "A few drops of water . . . an unseasonable cloud crossing the sky, sufficed for the overthrow of a world." In 1944 the Allied invasion of Normandy was made possible by a narrow interval of reasonably good weather between the bad. It was so narrow, in fact, that Supreme Allied Commander Dwight Eisenhower later expressed gratitude to "the gods of war." Paganism dies hard.

Every year brings fresh reminders of the weather's power over human life and events in the form of horrifying tornadoes, hurricanes and floods. These leave behind forgettable statistics and unforgettable images of devastated towns and battered humanity that can only humble people in the face of such wrath. Farmers often suffer the most, from the drought and plagues of biblical times to the hailstorms or quick freezes that even today can wipe out whole crops in minutes. Last week's icy assault on the Midwest, for all its ferocity and cost, is merely another reminder of the inescapable vulnerability of life and social well-being to the whims of the weather. And history is packed with reminders of far worse. The weather, for example, provoked a major social dislocation in the U.S. in the 1930s when it turned much of the Southwest into the Dust Bowl.

No wonder, then, that man's great dream has been some day to control the weather. The first step toward control, of course, is knowledge, and scientists have been hard at work for years trying to keep track of the weather. The U.S. and other nations have created an international apparatus that maintains some 100,000 stations to check the weather round the clock in every sector of the globe and, with satellites, in a good deal of the more than 4 billion cubic miles of the atmosphere. With computers on tap and electronic eyes in the sky, modern man has thus come far in dealing with the weather, alternately his nemesis and benefactor. Yet man's predicament today is not too far removed from that of his remote ancestors. For all the advances of scientific forecasting, in spite of the thousands of daily bulletins and advisories that get flashed about, the weather is still ultimately capricious and unpredictable. Man's dream of controlling it is still just that—a dream.

The very idea of control, in fact, raises enormous and troublesome questions. Who would decide what weather to program? Since weather patterns are interrelated, would interference cause harmful imbalances? Is weather that appears to be beneficial to man also beneficial to nature? The vision of scheduled weather also raises ambiguous feelings among the world's billions of weather fans—and poses at least one irresistible question: If weather were as predictable as holidays and eclipses, what in the world would everyone talk about?

—*TIME*, February 6, 1978

The Great American Cooling Machine

1979

"The greatest contribution to civilization in this century may well be air conditioning—and America leads the way." So wrote British Scholar-Politician S.F. Markham 32 years ago when a modern cooling system was still an exotic luxury. In a century that has yielded such treasures as the electric knife, spray-on deodorant and disposable diapers, anybody might question whether air conditioning is the supreme gift. There is not a whiff of doubt, however, that America is far out front in its use. As a matter of lopsided fact, the U.S. today, with a mere 5% of the population, consumes as much man-made coolness as the whole rest of the world put together.

Just as amazing is the speed with which this situation came to be. Air conditioning began to spread in industries as a production aid during World War II. Yet only a generation ago a chilled sanctuary during summer's stewing heat was a happy frill that ordinary people sampled only in movie houses. Today most Americans tend to take air conditioning for granted in homes, offices, factories, stores, theaters, shops, studios, schools, hotels and restaurants. They travel in chilled buses, trains, planes and private cars. Sporting events once associated with open sky and fresh air are increasingly boxed in and air cooled. Skiing still takes place outdoors, but such attractions as tennis, rodeos, football and, alas, even baseball are now often staged in synthetic climates like those of Houston's Astrodome and New Orleans' Superdome. A great many of the country's farming tractors are now, yup, air-conditioned.

It is thus no exaggeration to say that Americans have taken to mechanical cooling avidly and greedily. Many have become all but addicted, refusing to go places that are not air-conditioned. In Atlanta, shoppers in Lenox Square so resented having to endure natural heat while walking outdoors from chilled store to chilled store that the mall management enclosed and air-conditioned the whole sprawling shebang. The widespread whining about Washington's raising of thermostats to a mandatory 78°F suggests that people no longer think of interior coolness as an amenity but consider it a necessity, almost a birthright, like suffrage. The existence of such a view was proved last month when a number of federal judges, sitting too high and mighty to suffer 78°, defied and denounced the Government's energy-saving order to cut back on cooling. Significantly, there was no popular outrage at this judicial insolence; many citizens probably wished that they could be so highhanded.

Everybody by now is aware that the cost of the American way is enormous, that air conditioning is an energy glutton. It uses some 9% of all electricity produced. Such an extravagance merely to provide comfort is peculiarly American and strikingly at odds with all the recent rhetoric about national sacrifice in a period of menacing energy shortages. Other modern industrial nations such as Japan, Germany and France have managed all along to thrive with mere fractions of the man-made coolness used in the U.S., and precious little of that in private dwellings. Here, so profligate has its use become that the air conditioner is almost as glaring a symptom as the automobile of the national tendency to overindulge in every technical possibility, to use every convenience to such excess that the country looks downright coddled.

But not everybody is aware that high cost and easy comfort are merely two of the effects of the vast cooling of America. In fact air conditioning has substantially altered the country's character and folkways. With the dog days at hand and the thermostats ostensibly up, it is a good time to begin taking stock of what air conditioning has done besides lower the indoor temperature.

Many of its byproducts are so conspicuous that they are scarcely noticed. To begin with, air conditioning transformed the face of urban America by making possible those glassy, boxy, sealed-in skyscrapers on which the once humane geometries of places like San Francisco, Boston and Manhattan have been impaled. It has been indispensable, no less, to the functioning of sensitive advanced computers, whose high operating temperatures require that they be constantly cooled. Thus, in a very real way, air conditioning has made possible the ascendancy of computerized civilization. Its cooling protection has given rise not only to moon landings, space shuttles and Sky-labs but to the depersonalized punch-cardification of society that regularly gets people hot under the collar even in swelter-proof environments. It has also reshaped the national economy and redistributed political power simply by encouraging the burgeoning of the sultry southerly swatch of the country, profoundly influencing major migration trends of people and industry. Sunbelt cities like Phoenix, Atlanta, Dallas and Houston (where shivering indoor frigidity became a mark of status) could never have mushroomed so prosperously without air conditioning; some communities—Las Vegas in the Nevada desert and Lake Havasu City on the Arizona-California border—would shrivel and die overnight if it were turned off.

It has, as well, seduced families into retreating into houses with closed doors and shut windows, reducing the commonalty of neighborhood life and all but obsoleting the front-porch society whose open casual folkways were an appealing hallmark of a sweatier America. Is it really surprising that the public's often noted withdrawal into self-pursuit and privatism has coincided with the epic spread of air conditioning? Though science has little studied how habitual air conditioning affects mind or body, some medical experts suggest that, like other technical avoidance of natural swings in climate, air conditioning may take a toll on the human capacity to adapt to stress. If so, air conditioning is only like many other greatly useful technical developments that liberate man from nature by increasing his productivity and power in some ways—while subtly weakening him in others.

Neither scholars nor pop sociologists have really got around to charting and diagnosing all the changes brought about by air conditioning. Professional observers have for years been preoccupied with the social implications of the automobile and television. Mere glancing analysis suggests that the car and TV, in their most decisive influences on American habits, have been powerfully aided and abetted by air conditioning. The car may have created all those shopping centers in the boondocks, but only air conditioning has made them attractive to mass clienteles. Similarly, the artificial cooling of the living room undoubtedly helped turn the typical American into a year-round TV addict. Without air conditioning, how many viewers would endure reruns (or even Johnny Carson) on one of those pestilential summer nights that used to send people out to collapse on the lawn or to sleep on the roof?

Many of the side effects of air conditioning are far from being fully pinned down. It is a reasonable suspicion, though, that controlled climate, by inducing Congress to stay in Washington longer than it used to during the swelter season, thus presumably passing more laws, has contributed to bloated Government. One can only speculate that the advent of the supercooled bedroom may be linked to the carnal adventurism associated with the mid-century sexual revolution. Surely it is a fact—if restaurant complaints about raised thermostats are to be believed—that air conditioning induces at least expense-account diners to eat and drink more; if so, it must be credited with adding to the national fat problem.

Perhaps only a sophist might be tempted to tie the spread of air conditioning to the coincidentally rising divorce rate, but every attentive realist must have noticed that even a little window unit can instigate domestic tension and chronic bickering between couples composed of one who likes it on all the time and another who does not. In fact, perhaps surprisingly, not everybody likes air conditioning. The necessarily sealed rooms or buildings make some feel claustrophobic, cut off from the real world. The rush, whir and clatter of cooling units annoys others. There are even a few eccentrics who object to man-made cool simply because they like hot weather. Still, the overwhelming majority of Americans have taken to air conditioning like hogs to a wet wallow.

It might be tempting, and even fair, to chastise that vast majority for being spoiled rotten in their cool ascendancy. It would be more just, however, to observe that their great cooling machine carries with it a perpetual price tag that is going to provide continued and increasing chastisement during the energy crisis. Ultimately, the air conditioner, and the hermetic buildings it requires, may turn out to be a more pertinent technical symbol of the American personality than the car. While the car has been a fine sign of the American impulse to dart hither and yon about the world, the mechanical cooler more neatly suggests the maturing national compulsion to flee the natural world in favor of a technological cocoon.

Already architectural designers are toiling to find ways out of the technical trap represented by sealed buildings with immovable glass, ways that might let in some of the naturally cool air outside. Some have lately come up with a remarkable discovery: the openable window. Presumably, that represents progress.

—*TIME*, August 13, 1979

A New Distrust Of The Experts

1979

"Whenever the people are well informed, they can be trusted with their own government." Thomas Jefferson's axiom remains an indispensable premise of democracy. Yet the possibility of a sage and knowing public seems to be growing ever more elusive. Since the rise of science and technology as the commanding force in both government and social change, it has become harder and harder for most Americans to become really well informed on the problems they face as individuals or citizens. Such a trend is bound to raise questions about the future of popular rule.

Nowadays the very vocabulary of public discourse can be bewildering. Even to be half informed, the American-on-the-street must grasp terms like deoxyribonucleic acid, fantastic prospects like genetic engineering and bizarre phenomena like nuclear meltdown. The technical face of things has driven some people into a bored sort of cop-out—"science anxiety," it is called by Physics Professor Jeffry Mallow of Loyola University in Chicago. The predicament has made most Americans hostage to the superior knowledge of the expert: the scientist, the technician, the engineer, the specialist.

Society has grown so complicated that there is renewed interest in the possibility of a "science court" that might deal impartially with arcane controversy. It has grown so technical that some lawyers wonder whether ordinary electors can still adequately function as jurors. Says Attorney Gary Ahrens, a professor at the University of Iowa: "Practically nothing is commonsensical any more." Surely the spectacle of the public making decisions in semi-darkness is an affront to common sense.

Dependency on the experts seemed tenable in the more innocent era when science was viewed as a virtually infallible cornucopia of social goodies. Americans long clung to Virgil's ancient advice: "Believe an expert." Today, however, Americans are no longer willing to acquiesce gratefully in either the discoveries of science or their application. The citizen has rediscovered that the best of experts will now and then launch an unsinkable *Titanic*.

The public has needed no expertise to read about DDT, thalidomide and cyclamates, nor to learn that the DES that seemed a nifty preventive of miscarriage in the 1950s was being linked to cancer a generation later. The citizen's problem, at bottom, is how to assess the things that so often come forth in the beguiling guise of blessings. What to believe? Whom to trust? This is a recipe for public frustration.

The shadow of science falls across decisions common to daily existence. Is this medication safe? Is forgoing sugar worth the hazards of saccharin? Are the conveniences of the Pill worth raising the risk of circulatory disease? The uncertain answers come from product analysts, dietitians, pharmacists, lawyers, physicians. American society, as Federal Trade Commission Chairman Michael Pertschuk puts it, has become "dominated by professionals who call us 'clients' and tell us of our 'needs.'"

The biggest problem, however, is that the faith of the American people in the experts has been badly shaken. People have learned, for one thing, that certified technical gospel is far from immortal. Medicine changes its mind about tonsillectomies that used to be routinely performed. Those dazzling phosphate detergents turn out to be anathema to the environment. Scarcely a week goes by without the credibility of one expert or another falling afoul of some spike of fresh news. (Just last week an array of nonprescription sedatives used by millions was linked, through the ingredient methapyrilene, to cancer.) Moreover, experts are constantly challenging experts, debating the benefits and hazards of virtually every technical thrust. Who knows anything for sure? Could supersonic aircraft truly damage the ozone? The technical sages disagree.

Thus the problems that the individual copes with as a private person are knotty enough; public issues have grown immeasurably more complex. Government has long since subsumed science and technology into its realm, both as the fountainhead of its projects and as an object of its regulation. The calculations that measure national military strength are as impenetrable to the civilian-on-the-street as the formulas of the ancient alchemists. The surreal arithmetic of SALT might as well be the music of the spheres, for all the help it gives ordinary folks trying to get a clear picture of the country's real and relative strengths. The nervous strategist is not the only one to covet verification; the common citizen could also use some.

Then, too, much information crucial to the personal and social decisions of citizens is methodically hidden or withheld. The scientific world has always tended to hoard lore on work in progress, and the Government's customary secrecy in military matters, intelligence and foreign affairs has spread to many parts of the bureaucratic and corporate spheres. The clandestine spirit that properly cloaked the devising of atomic weapons inevitably carried over to veil the development of nuclear power for civilian purposes.

The result of secrecy compounded by confusion and some startling ignorance was dramatized by the Three Mile Island nuclear power plant crisis. While the event made plain that Government and corporate experts had not quite leveled with the public about the hazards of nuclear power, it also proved, frighteningly enough, that the experts sometimes did not tell the whole story simply because they did not know it.

Joseph M. Hendrie, chairman of the Nuclear Regulatory Commission, said of himself and other officials, as they tried to cope with an incipient meltdown: "We are operating . . . like a couple of blind men staggering around making decisions."

Intentional deception sometimes leaves the citizenry in a plight as awkward as Hendrie's. Last month a former ranking employee charged that the Hooker Chemicals and Plastics Corp. of Niagara Falls, New York, had kept workers in the dark about the hazards of toxic chemicals they dealt with. Federal atomic authorities, it was disclosed last month, were encouraged by President Dwight Eisenhower to confuse the public about the risks of radiation fallout during the atomic bomb tests in Nevada in the 1950s; Government officials refused to warn inhabitants of nearby regions that they were absorbing possibly lethal doses of radiation.

The citizenry's essential interest is not in knowledge *per se* but the social uses to which it is put. What is often kept from the citizen, in the form of knowledge, is social and political power. When demonstrations and controversies break out over seemingly esoteric technical questions, the underlying question, as Cornell University's Dorothy Nelkin puts it in a paper on "Science as a Source of Political Conflict," is always the same: "Who should control crucial policy choices?" Such choices, she adds, tend to stay in the hands of those who control "the context of facts and values in which policies are shaped."

On its face, the situation may help explain the mood of public disenchantment that has persisted long after the events—Viet Nam and Watergate—that were supposed to have caused it. Surely neither of those national traumas caused the drop of popular confidence in almost all key U.S. institutions that Pollster Louis Harris recently recorded. It also seems doubtful that either deprived the Administration's energy crusade of both popular support and belief. Could it be that many citizens simply feel foreclosed not only from knowledge but also from the power that knowledge would give them?

The public itself, it must be admitted, bears a fair share of responsibility for its dilemma. It has usually welcomed the advances and conveniences—swift travel, cheap energy, life-prolonging medication, magical cosmetics—and left itself no choice but to live with the inherent risks it does not so cheerfully accept. A completely risk-free society would be a dead society. In today's increasingly risk-shy atmosphere, the public may tend to exaggerate some of the dangers at hand. Indeed, it may be swinging from too much awe of the "miracles" of science and technology to excessive skepticism about them. In reality, the public has always wanted to lean on the experts—until they have failed, or seemed to.

It is fair to suppose that even if the public had access to all knowledge about everything, there would still be a good deal of befuddlement and groping. Not many have the ability, energy and will to bone up on every issue. If it is reasonable for Americans to demand more candor, prudence—and humility—from the experts, it is also reasonable that the citizenry demand of itself ever greater diligence in using all available information, including journalism's increasingly technical harvest.

Plainly the citizen's plight is not subject to quickie remedy. Yet any solution would have to entail a shift in the relationship between the priests of knowledge and the lay public. The expert will have to play a more conscious role as citizen, just as the ordinary American will have to become ever more a student of technical lore. The learned elite will doubtless remain indispensable. Still, the fact that they are exalted over the public should not mean that they are excused from responsibility to it—not unless the Jeffersonian notion of popular self-rule is to be lost by default.

—*TIME,* May 14, 1979

Living Happily Against The Odds

1979

"All you need to do to become ill in our modern world is to follow ordinary patterns of diet and life-style."
—Dr. Charles T. McGee

Inflation. Recession. Iran. Cuba. Unemployment. Taxes. Et cetera. Et cetera. Given the number, gravity and persistence of their country's problems, Americans obviously need occasional relief from national worries so that they can at least try to enjoy their lives as individuals. Yet it has become harder and harder for people to find anything to do or use that does not come with some built-in anxiety. The trouble is that everywhere they turn these days, one thing or another is posted with the red flag of danger, if not with the skull and crossbones of mortal horror.

Such is the impression created by America's all-purpose early alert system. Day after day the air bleats and print blinks with warnings and alarms. Cancer alerts have become almost as commonplace as weather reports. Strictures on how to avoid heart attacks pop up everywhere. Preventive campaigns stir up a constant din of sermons against careless driving, against starting fires, against getting too fat. It is like the continual murmur of doom's own voice.

The symphony of warnings even has elaborate seasonal variations. Christmas, for instance, is the time to avoid giving little Johnny toys that can maim or pajamas treated with carcinogenic flameproofing. But every season brings fresh cautions against some new menacing gunk found in air, water, food, medicines. This year alerts were raised about stuffs used to treat dandruff, insomnia, alcoholism and high blood pressure.

Clearly, the U.S. is now buffeted by a public atmosphere that has grown chronically and pervasively cautionary. Apprehensive outcries wail forth from broadcasts, newspapers, magazines, posters, labels, environmental journals, medical tracts, Government reports, even books. One of the books is a brand-new broadside by Dr. Charles T. McGee, a clinical ecologist of Alamo, California, who is quoted above. His 220-page polemic issues a general alarm about multifarious dangers that lurk in every nook and cranny of contemporary civilization. Even fluorescent lighting, he says, may, in some weird way, weaken the muscles. The book, billed as a "crash course in protecting your health from hidden hazards of modern living," is entitled *How to Survive Modern Technology*. Anybody with a frail heart might not even survive the book.

Admittedly, modern times are fraught with real hazards and no sensible person would sniff at prudent precautions. Still it is hard not to shudder at the sheer volume of disquieting cautions, at the constancy, variety and intensity of the fearful clamor. Indeed, one may reasonably wonder whether the very climate of alarm itself has not become a hazard to health and serenity.

Everybody's psyche now takes a drubbing day in and out from the concatenations of danger. An American can scarcely make a move nowadays without being pushed into a state of alert. Warnings about nutrients left out of the diet are as grave as those about pollutants included. Scotch and beer have joined the list of potables that may contain dangerous chemicals. So has mother's milk, in which PCBs have turned up. Birth defects could be linked to caffeine from coffee or any source, it was reported just last month. Even peanut butter, as an occasional bearer of aflatoxin, has been flagged as a menace. Driving? Fasten the seat belt—unless discouraged by warnings that most of them do not work. On the road, even rest-room signs often gratuitously warn against VD. Flying? Remember that some passengers get ozone poisoning in those high-altitude supersonic jets. Sleeping? Doing it too little or too much is associated with shortened life spans. Prettying up? It seems that some hair dyes among other cosmetics, contain malignant agents. Need exercise? Take heed that middle-aged joggers are constantly falling dead on the side roads. Feeling sickly? Steer clear of surgery-mongering doctors. Taking a pill? Make sure it will not hook you. Worried about cancer? That very worry may cause cancer, some say. Anybody thinking of fleeing might peruse another recent book, this one by Dr. Robert A. Shakman. Its title: *Where You Live May Be Hazardous to Your Health*. Its implicit message: You can't escape.

Enough. A complete list of warnings would fill a shelf of books. Plainly the 20th century has turned into the Age of Admonition. It is also clear that the atmosphere is distributing more than a bit of anxiety. A modern form of morbid gallows humor ("Life is hazardous to your health"; "Everything causes cancer") has now become the respectable coin of small talk.

Only a recluse could fail to know somebody who uses less ingenuity in living than in worrying and guarding against subtle hazards. Perhaps the surest sign that the admonitory mood is taking a toll is the fact that Americans have begun to write advice columnists about the problems that all the cautions cause. Warnings about cholesterol in eggs, nitrate in bacon, caffeine in coffee (and, a while back, risky chemicals in even the decaffeinated variety) have sapped the fun out of eating breakfast for some people, it seems. Wrote one such: "I'd try bread and water, but I'm pretty sure that as soon as I begin to enjoy it, I'll find out it's bad for me."

Such hangdog pathos is enough to provoke wistful dreams of returning to the vanished day when a person was guided only by folk wisdom: an apple a day would keep the doctor away. But there is no going back. Today the apple must be checked for sprayed-on toxins. The alarm system is here to stay. It would be foolhardy as well as foolish to suggest that it be shut down; it is, in truth, indispensable for guiding those who wish guidance. What is needed is a strategy for getting through life passably happy despite all the ominous background chatter.

Though sophisticates have long sneered at him, Norman Vincent Peale, who said that "you do not need to be a victim of worry," was not entirely wrong. Thinkers more serious than Peale have construed a fearful attitude as a danger in itself. Jesus of Nazareth advised against fretting even about tomorrow. Psychologist William James saw life itself as a process of risk taking and thought it was debilitating to take risks too much to heart. He urged people to will themselves to be confident of survival, to pretend confidence if necessary, allowing not even the "sweet" cautions of scientists to undermine them.

Cynics may shrug at doctrines of willful optimism. Still, Americans have a right to be optimistic. After all, they are living longer and longer. Perhaps each new alarm should be coupled with a dire warning that life is likely to go on despite all the dangers.

—TIME, December 24, 1979

THREE

On Leading The Cheers For No. 1

The Human Need To Break Records

The Bull Market In Personal Secrets

There Must Be A Nicer Way

Hard Times For The Status-Minded

The Game Of The Name

Time To Reflect On Blah-Blah-Blah

So You Want To Be A Journalist

On Leading The Cheers For No. 1

1981

The first right on earth is the right of the ego.
—Ayn Rand

With her usual authoritarian sweep, Author Ayn Rand strikes a basic blow for her consistent dogma of individualism. Though she is more a cult figure than a popular philosopher, her words mirror an attitude that is becoming more and more common in the U.S., particularly among public figures. Indeed, an increasing number of Americans seem to have concluded that the right to ego implies the duty to exercise it publicly. The result is something of a rout for the time-honored American taboo against tooting one's own horn. Today it is commonplace for Americans to come right out and admit just how wonderful they really are.

Listen to the new surge of self-applause. Television's Howard Cosell ranks himself as a sports commentator: "I really believe I'm the best. My relationship with the men who play the games—all games—is probably unparalleled in this country." Private Citizen Joan Kennedy assesses herself for a *Ladies' Home Journal* interviewer: "I have talent. I know I'm smart. I got straight A's in graduate school. I've still got my looks. I know I've got all these terrific things going for me. I mean, my God, you are talking to, I think, one of the most fascinating women in this country." *Sugar Babies* Star Mickey Rooney makes clear he knows all there is to know about theatrics: "I'm 58 years in the theater. Nobody gives me instructions."

Baseball Player Reggie Jackson speaks of his importance to his sport: "I am the straw that stirs the drink. It all comes back to me." Chrysler Chief Lee Iacocca recalls what happened to him while he was rising in the business world: "I got pretty damn good." Chicago Realty Mogul Evangeline Gouletas awards herself an ovation on the eve of marrying Governor Hugh Carey of New York: "In Chicago, they love me. In Chicago, I am already First Lady." Novelist Gore Vidal confides why the New York *Times* published a favorable review of his new book *Creation*: "They're desperate for me to write for them."

Bleats of unchecked egoism are now so commonplace that self-glorification may be well on the way to becoming standard American style. Yet such an epidemic of flagrant braggadocio would have scandalized the country not long ago. Most Americans have always felt, as many still feel, dutybound to sniff at the ostentatious chest thumper and look down on all public boasting. Brazen self-admiration has never been considered criminal, nor necessarily degenerate, but it has always been judged tacky—poor form, at best. Good form has always required reticence about one's virtues. To think well of oneself was one thing, but, under the traditional rules, it was quite another to give voice to one's privately cultivated self-esteem. Indeed, even if somebody else called attention to one's admirable points, one was supposed to disclaim the praise.

The braggart, of course, has always been present on the American scene, and boasting has been tolerated when it happened to come from certain types—poets, entertainers, politicians—who were considered beyond the pale anyhow. It was all right for Walt Whitman to indulge his flagrant self celebration ("I dote on myself, there is that lot of me and all so luscious") because, as a poet, he was lost to gentility anyway. The public similarly has always recognized that in a democracy, where candidates for elective office have to sell themselves like consumer goods, politicians have little practical choice but to depict themselves as heaven's gift to the voter. Still, for most people, self-containment has long been thought a virtue.

The old ideal probably had begun to fade when Norman Mailer published a hodgepodge of fiction and autobiography under the title *Advertisements for Myself.* In any case, windy self-advertisement became more and more popular in the years that followed. Said John Lennon at the peak of the Beatles' popularity: "We're more popular than Jesus Christ now." Said Heavyweight Boxer Muhammad Ali, in a typical flight: "It ain't no accident that I'm the greatest man in the world at this time in history." The same period at last produced an intellectual model for publicly saluting the self: *Commentary* Editor Norman Podhoretz's autobiographical book *Making It.* Wrote Podhoretz: "I looked upon those who possessed . . . fame, and I liked what I saw; I measured myself against them, and I did not fall short."

The ideal of modesty, though hardly dead, has begun to seem almost quaint. In an age when some observers think the U.S. has entered the "culture of narcissism," in the words of Christopher Lasch's study, many people think that self-effacement is tainted with hypocrisy. Says Economist John Kenneth Galbraith in his new memoir *A Life in Our Times*: "Truth is not always coordinate with modesty." Perhaps, but then, truth is *never* coordinate with vanity. Self-praise is inescapably distorted and corrupted at its source, and this—not some arbitrary convention of etiquette—makes the self-praiser always seem at least ridiculous or fraudulent, and often worse. One must return to Reinhold Neibuhr for the key: "Since the self judges itself by its own standards, it finds itself good."

The standard of modesty evolved out of concerns deeper than ephemeral questions of style and etiquette. The discipline of reining in one's tendency to boast is, after all, merely part of the larger discipline of keeping the ego in check.

And why should anyone wish to do that? Simply because the main thing that traps people into spiritual emptiness is some sort of berserk ego. Says Psychologist Shirley Sugerman in *Sin and Madness: Studies in Narcissism*: "The ancient wisdom of both East and West [tells] repeatedly of man's tendency to self-idolatry, self-encapsulation, and its result: self-destruction."

Nobody need suppose that a bit of windy conceit is going to add up to self-destruction. Still, everybody knows at heart that boasting usually signals some pathetic private weaknesses. Psychology has never been mystified by braggadocio. Says Associate Director John Schimel of the William A. White Institute of Psychiatry: "It is a way of denying some form of insecurity." The rule is simple: the louder and more prolonged the bragging, the more profound and painful the secret doubts and distances that are being masked. Given this pattern, the self-glorifier deserves less than applause and more than mockery. Pity is perhaps the appropriate response.

—*TIME*, June 8, 1981

The Human Need To Break Records

1980

When Albuquerque Businessman Maxie Anderson, 45, and his son Kris, 23, completed the first nonstop transcontinental balloon flight in May, the four-day voyage of 2,818 miles from Fort Baker, California, to Ste. Felicite, Quebec, set a world record for overland flight. Another, more esoteric record was achieved in April by Jerry Dietrick, 56, of Florence, Kentucky, who became the first pilot to fly solo from Cincinnati to London to Munich in a single-engine plane of the 3,850-lb. to 6,414-lb. class.

Such record-setting news scratches up a brief twitch of public interest and a flurry of deserved hurrahs. Yet the tidings of singular achievement seem less and less to arouse genuine excitement. New records come along so frequently, and in so many categories, that it is impossible to work up the appropriate celebratory mood for every one of them. The exceptional is in danger of becoming commonplace.

Three volunteers at Duke University in Durham, North Carolina, set a world record this spring when they spent 28 days in a pressure tank to simulate a dive 2,132 ft. into the sea. To raise money for the American Heart Association, Ohio State University students played a 4,378-seat game of musical chairs last month and broke the old record of 3,728 chairs.

The business of setting and topping records has got completely out of hand in the 20th century. Merely keeping track of records requires the toil of a considerable industry and the regular publication of hundreds of thick books with fine print. Scores of thousands of new records are claimed every year. There would be a surfeit even if the world of sports did not chip in its promiscuous confetti of records.

And quasi records: Pete Rose of the Philadelphia Phillies walked and then stole his way around the bases a few games ago, becoming the first National League player to do that since Harvey Hendrick of Brooklyn in 1928.
Every other day somebody does something that has never been done before. Or else repeats some improbable feat—only faster, deeper, higher, with different equipment or at a different age. The act of dying is one of the very few human activities that do not stir up competitive fever among people. "After Sir Edmund Hillary," says Boston *Globe* Columnist M.R. Montgomery, "you can climb Everest on a pogo stick without attracting envy or admiration." But, in fact, once the notion of climbing a mountain by pogo stick has been conceived, it would not be surprising if somebody had a go at it.

At 57, Coca-Cola Heiress Frances Woodruff of Atlanta is said to be the oldest woman ever to ride and fly a hang glider. In Pampa, Texas, Plumber Ronnie Farmer, 29, ate 100 hot jalapeno peppers in 15 minutes, destroying the previous record (94 in 111 minutes) and probably his innards as well. In Japan, Hideaki Tomoyori has learned to carry the mathematical formulation pi (3.141 etc.) to 20,000 places, putting to shame his own earlier record of 15,151 places.

It was not always this way. While it is true that St. Simeon the Younger, the 6th century Syrian monk, perched on a stone pillar for 45 years, he did it not to claim a record but to elevate his soul. It was not until late in the 19th century that the notion of *setting* a record even occurred in sports literature. Only in the 20th has record-consciousness grown into a worldwide obsession. Scholars say that record keeping took hold mainly because of the scientific revolution's tendency to quantify and rank everything. The preoccupation with records, and the breaking thereof, pervaded sports early in this century and spread, much too quickly, to virtually every other field of endeavor.

A North Carolina youth, Lang Martin, holds the record for balancing golf balls vertically: he stacked up six of them. A Northeast Louisiana University student, Arden Chapman, caught in his mouth a grape thrown the longest distance—259 ft.

It is easy to understand the performer's urge to do the improbable, the difficult, the unique, the best. Claiming a record, any record, provides massage to the ego, varnish for the pride and a tic of celebrity. To hold a record, in the words of Allen Guttmann, professor of American Studies at Amherst College, "is a uniquely modern form of immortality."

Johann Heinrich Karl Thieme of Aldenburg, Germany, dug a record 23,311 graves during a 50-year career as a sexton. Though he entered his own, final resting place in 1826, he lives on—if nowhere else—in the Guinness Book of World Records.

The *Guinness Book* is proof that spectators, no less than performers, have been thoroughly infected with the obsession of recorditis. The public avidly eats up records of just about everything on earth: the biggest or highest or fastest or heaviest or deepest or oddest of natural or manmade wonders. Just such a smorgasbord is what the *Guinness Book* has offered since it first came out in 1955. It has now sold 40 million copies in 23 languages worldwide, 25 million in the U.S. alone.

Inspired by Mark Gottlieb of Olympia, Washington, who set a record for playing the violin under water, Japan has come up with an entire underwater orchestra, a first. To raise funds for a local charity, a man and a woman in Des Moines lovingly sat in tubs of vanilla pudding for 24hr.34min.20sec., the only record ever set for a pudding sit—but one that will no doubt be challenged.

The urge to do something better, something distinct, is the very essence of human nature. Constant individual competition is only one manifestation of the impulse that is, in its deeper workings, nothing less than the engine for the advancement of the species. This was no doubt so even in unrecorded ages. Now that society has become so proficient at keeping records as a way of celebrating the competitive trait, it is no wonder that people get so carried away in the making and breaking of them. Moreover, the likelihood is that in the future, well . . .

Stanley Cottrell, 37, of Atlanta sprinted out of New York City in mid-May, intending to run the 3,049 miles to San Francisco somewhat faster than the 53 days that it took Irishman Tom McGrath in 1977. One wondered whether Cottrell's path might cross that of Joe Bowen, 36, who is currently walking on stilts from California to Kentucky, and has already broken the distance record set by another stiltwalker who strode 1,830 miles on the sticks from Paris to Moscow in 1891.

The future thus seems clear. The reaching for new records will never let up. Moreover, it should not be put down just because it leads to some ridiculous results. It would make as little sense to disparage the artistic impulse only because it produces, along with much that is noble, a great deal that is silly.

In the end, the constant striving of people to do better than others—or than themselves—arises out of whatever sets the human species apart. All creatures compete, but for most the contest is only for the food and space to survive, to hold their own. Only humans striving for more than mere survival have elaborated competitiveness into the cultural imperative that it is. The obsession with setting records is finally inextricable from the human determination to rise above the past.

—*TIME*, June 16, 1980

THE BULL MARKET IN PERSONAL SECRETS

1980

In those days I think she'd experiment sexually with anything and she was absolutely open about it.

—*Tallulah, Darling,*
by Denis Brian

I told Marlon to hurry and get all his clothes together and go up on the roof because I didn't know whether Burt would come back up the elevator or run up the stairs.

—*Shelley,*
by Shelley Winters

Tidbits of such an odor would have caused gasps if they had been mentioned in private chats not long ago, or full-blown scandals if they had appeared in print. Today nobody bothers to lift an eyebrow at the seamiest intimate tale, not even when it is about the life of a President. The reason is plain: tidings of intimate goings-on have become as common as junk food in the U.S. In fact, the country has developed what looks like an enduring bull market in personal secrets.

Tattletale stories have always been around, true, but never so numerously, so brazenly, so unrelentingly as today. The personal travails and bedroom vagaries of real people are blared forth in newspapers and magazines, on television and in movies. Biographies and autobiographies about and by celebrities actually deliver the shadowy scandals that fan magazines used to promise in misleading blurbs. And so many books are rattling once closeted skeletons that even gamy chronicles about the likes of Tallulah and Shelley have to fight for attention. Ordinary Americans, moreover, tend increasingly to litter casual small talk with personal secrets of a sort that only priests and the most trusted confidants once enjoyed. The public traffic in what used to be respected as intimate lore is conspicuous and feverish enough to have provoked some thought about the implications of the trend. Something more than a mere departure from decorum must be involved when a society begins to live habitually in a blizzard of under-the-rug sweepings. Only the simple-minded could shrug it off as nothing more than a side effect of the open and permissive social mode that emerged in the 1960s. Letting it all hang out may be refreshing and even healthy, but not under all circumstances; neither honesty nor candor requires that anybody's, let alone everybody's, intimate life be ventilated on the village green. The booming commerce in intimacies is extraordinary if only because U.S. society so strongly cherished the personal preserve in the past. The American's home may still be his castle, but given the drift of things, it is easy to imagine that a peering, leering crowd is gathered at the window.

The personally sacred realm used to enclose a great deal that went on at home and at large; there were reasons for confidentiality between doctor and patient. But the variety of intimate matters now bandied about is without apparent limits. On talk shows like Phil Donahue's, ordinary people regularly recount stories of emotional disturbance, marital discord, incest. Men chat about their vasectomies, women about their hysterectomies. The spectacle of Lyndon B. Johnson flashing his surgical scar to the world, so vulgar at the time, seems comparatively genteel in retrospect.

The revelatory fever has only recently reached an epidemic scale. Only seven years ago, Americans were astonished, shocked and dismayed—as well as fascinated—when public television presented *An American Family,* an exhibition of the personal trials and griefs of the family of Bill and Pat Loud, including their on-the-air breakup. But the Loud show's tell-all mode clearly proved infectious. Since then, the traffic in intimate secrets has become almost a staple of popular entertainment. Consider:

In *Bittersweet,* Actress Susan Strasberg tattles about her adolescent affair with Actor Richard Burton, and exposes gritty drug-fueled scenes from her marriage to Actor Christopher Jones. In *Haywire,* a memoir that has become a TV film, Brooke Hayward (daughter of Actress Margaret Sullavan and Producer Leland Hayward) immortalizes a family history of divorce, breakdown, suicide. In *Mommie Dearest,* Christina Crawford depicts her mother, Actress Joan Crawford, as a promiscuous lush given to brutal child abuse. In *I'm Dancing as Fast as I Can,* TV Producer Barbara Gordon publicizes the story of her addiction to Valium. In *Memoir of a Gambler,* Playwright Jack Richardson details his flings with Las Vegas whores. Rhythm and Blues Singer Marvin Gaye has even turned the bitter themes of a painful 14-year marriage into a hit record album, *Here, My Dear.* Author-Director Bob Fosse has let it be known that his own life is echoed in his film *All That Jazz,* a tale about a lecherous choreographer.

The demand for exposed intimacies is easier to understand than the supply. The public hunger for spilled beans is just more of the craving for news, the yen to be titillated, touched or amused by the foibles and agonies of others. Squalid and sleazy tales may reinforce the smug superiority of the righteous or provide perverse comfort for the miscreant. But Americans of all stripes have always had, though not uniquely, what University of Chicago Law Professor Philip Kurland calls a "public commitment to voyeurism." Still, why is the voyeuristic hunger suddenly being so abundantly pandered to? Why are so many people revealing personal secrets so casually?

The wish for money and attention stands at the top of a confusion of reasons. Yet venality and exhibitionism together do not account satisfactorily for the eruption of personal intimacies that marks this era, no more than simple curiosity can account for the greedy consumption of them. The traffic in intimacies may be a naive, if elaborate, response to the generalized loneliness and isolation that are characteristic of the times: it may represent a form of sharing, though a desperate form. Many psychologists attest that lonely people have an extra-special wish to know what other lives are like, and that those who disclose their inner lives basically crave acceptance. Public confession has increased, says University of Chicago Theologian Martin Marty, as the popular sense of God has diminished. Says Marty: "When you can't talk to God, you've got to tell a million people." That insight parallels one offered by Sociology Professor Todd Gitlin of the University of California at Berkeley: "The public has become the new priesthood of the confessional."

The trend, finally, suggests the working of human currents more fundamental than a shift in manners and mores. Serious observers have long worried about the capacity of modern technical civilization to manipulate mass society partly by exposing and trivializing personal values that were once held secret and sacred. Twenty-six years ago, in fact, French Sociologist Jacques Ellul, in *The Technological Society*, forecast: "Our deepest instincts and our most secret passions will be analyzed, published, and exploited." The great eruption of secrets is, finally, more than amazing. It is also a bit ominous.

—*TIME*, July 14, 1980

There Must Be A Nicer Way

1981

The question comes from the Rev. Donald Wildmon, head of the National Federation for Decency: "Where is the TV show about a modern home with decent people?" The glib answer is: Nowhere. Ordinarily, a crusade to purify the tales shown on the tube would deserve only that short shrift. But Wildmon's question begs for a more thoughtful response, if only because TV's gory and jiggly tales are not the only ones that are conspicuously short on niceness. The same can be said of most all the world's fiction, narrative or dramatic, trash or quality.

True, ostensibly decent people turn up now and then in literature, but they almost never get depicted as being swept away by impulses to sweetness. They are more often set up for a comedown. On one end of the literary spectrum, Hamlet might have been a pleasant fellow if Shakespeare had not handicapped him with that belief in ghosts, plus suicidal and homicidal tendencies. On the other end, given the way authors are, Jack is bound to wind up falling all over himself every time he tries to fetch a pail of water. In truth, the world's literary and theatrical output, from high drama to nursery rhymes, is as violent and vice-ridden as yesterday's news. Poet Ezra Pound may have had something of the sort in mind when he said: "Literature is news that stays news."

Storytellers, like journalists, have never been much for emphasizing the sweet, the decent, the well behaved. Odysseus, to pluck an early example from Homer, was a wife-neglecting troublemaker if there ever was one. Even in the inspired stories of the Bible, people seldom behave very well, beginning with Adam and Eve and proceeding to Cain and Abel and the folk in Sodom and Gomorrah. Contemporary fictions create their own mischief: Portnoy, for example, spends precious little time collecting for the United Fund.

Can nothing be done, then, to satisfy what might be called the niceness market? Surprisingly the answer is yes, something *could* be done. Somebody *could* produce a Literature of Niceness to supplement the not-so-nice real thing. In a society that is overloaded with writers, there must be imagination enough to contrive sunnier alternative life-styles for many of the fictional characters who otherwise will endure in the pain, anguish and futile passion imagined by their authors. Why, for one instance, shouldn't King Lear be seen in some truly golden retirement years, preferably in an adults-only community? And why not a tale in which Othello and Desdemona kiss and make up? Imagine Lady Macbeth joining the Gray Ladies. Or Molly Bloom enrolling in needlepoint class. Or Sir Clifford Chatterley making a successful pilgrimage to Lourdes.

Could not *Heart of Darkness* be offset by *Heart of Lightness*, in which Marlow narrates how the kindly Mr. Kurtz dedicated himself voluntarily to training the tribes along the Nile in personal hygiene? Might not *The Call of The Wild* be counterbalanced by *The Call of The Tame*, in which a big, clumsy, good-natured dog named Buck goes on a tour of Hollywood homes, including Lassie's? Who could be offended if *An American Tragedy* spun off a happy shadow called *An American Comedy*, in which Clyde Griffiths saves his girlfriend Roberta from drowning and receives a $7.50 reward from the grateful foreman of the factory in which Roberta is considered irreplaceable? Another natural would be *Life of a Salesman*, in which Willy Loman, 63, invited to take early retirement by his company, finds fulfillment in the neighborhood shuffleboard league.

Indeed, the entire subject merits serious attention. What is clearly needed is a Five-Foot Shelf of Nice Stories. Some initial possibilities:

The Brothers Karamazov. Dmitri, Ivan and Alyosha Karamazov give Daddy a surprise Father's Day party.

Dr. Jekyll and Mr. Hyde. A good doctor stumbles onto a magical chemical that transforms him into an even better Mr. Hyde, in which guise he organizes fellow townsmen into a bandage-rolling society.

Oliver Twist. A patriotic English boy contributes to prosperity by going on a low-fat, low-protein, low-carbohydrate diet.

Dr. Faustus. Tempted by the devil, the doctor, a chiropractor, finds that temptation rubs him the wrong way and so gives the devil a quick brush-off.

Dracula. An affable count of the title achieves celebrity status in his Transylvania community by becoming the first citizen to show up when the new blood bank holds its first blood-donation day.

Anna Karenina. A pretty young Russian matron gets a certain Count Vronsky interested in stamp collecting and so saves him from wasting his life in passion and frivolity.

The Picture of Dorian Gray. An adventurous young man takes up painting and captures the essence of evil in one great portrait.

Uncle Tom's Cabin. Generous Uncle Tom designs and builds a play cabin in the backyard for his favorite niece Eliza.

Tobacco Road. The people in a small Georgia town throw their tobacco products into the main street after Jeeter Lester and his family persuade them to give up smoking, chewing and dipping.

Madame Bovary. Emma, a young Frenchwoman, finds contentment in marriage and work with the Welcome Wagon.

Appointment in Samarra. A young American husband succeeds in pulling himself out of a sulk in time to keep a date with the orthodontist.

Still, one may wonder whether this kind of story has much pulling power. The human spectator's time-tested preference for the un-nice in stories and drama may be obvious, but the reasons for it are surely not. Aristotle, with an eye on formal tragedy, believed that by identification with the anguished souls onstage, spectators could purge themselves of burdensome emotions buried in real life. William Faulkner more than once said that he created characters in violent circumstances in an effort to get at "the truth of the human heart," and it may be that, many readers and viewers of fiction have some kindred goal.

It was left for Leo Tolstoy to underscore most aptly the mundane reason for mankind's taste in viewing and reading. Wrote he: "Happy families are all alike; every unhappy family is unhappy in its own way." Niceness, in other words, however admired in real life, is inherently repetitious and boring as a subject of fiction. Is it possible that the very weakness that makes the human species difficult if not evil is the main thing that makes it interesting? If so, that is scarcely the only contradiction in the human drama. Alas, one may, plausibly enough, wonder whether humankind, if it had remained in Eden, might not have perished of ennui.

—*TIME*, July 20, 1981

Hard Times For The Status-Minded

1981

He may never have been a Galileo of the social firmament but as a journalist Vance Packard is clear-eyed enough to have seen, before anybody else, that the post-World War II U.S. had got caught up in a compulsive competition for status. The proof came in *The Status Seekers* (1959), a dissection of those Americans who, as the author put it, were "continually straining to surround themselves with visible evidence of the superior rank they are claiming." Since that happened to include just about the entire U.S. population, the great status game, once focused, provoked a great many fears that it would damage the egalitarian ideal and hasten the evolution of sharp class lines. What none of the fearful saw was that, given the services of mass production and sustained prosperity, universal chasing after prestige would engender such a gorgeous and gaudy muddle of status symbols as to reduce the game to farce—which it has now plainly become.

Status in its diverse forms still exists, no doubt, and many an American is still out there grabbing after some of it. What makes the spectacle ridiculous now is that, except in rare cases, people who have latched onto some status cannot be sure of how to flash the news to the world, and people who are watching cannot be sure who is dramatizing what sort of status with what symbol. Order Gucci loafers and you only risk winding up shod the same way as the boy who delivers them. A Cadillac today signifies nothing about the owner except that he might well pull in at the next Burger King. Incontrovertibly, any game has been seriously maimed when you can no longer tell who is winning or losing. The status game had surely begun to turn absurd as soon as the man in the gray flannel suit began turning up in denim and sneakers—with no loss of prestige. The absurdity had clearly become utter by the year now ending: it was the year in which the President of the U.S. had to resort to the jelly bean for a symbol that set him apart from other folks.

The present symbolic muddle is enough to make one nostalgic for the good old days when everybody imagined that he could peg a person's status with only a few facts about the subject's clothes, schooling, job, neighborhood and car. The days when everybody enjoyed the habit of looking at all the artifacts of civilized existence as though they were primarily badges of rank. The days when elitist Middle Americans casually sneered at fellow citizens who lived in suburban split-level houses—which only a Rockefeller could afford today. Inflation is just one of the things that undermined the great status chase. The prior years of sustained prosperity contributed to the same end—giving people of middling status possession of most of the fashions and products (luxury gadgetry, stereos, color TV sets) that only the well-heeled could afford formerly. Then, too, the cultural conniptions of the 1960s and '70s helped subvert the rules of the status game; hell-raising youth provided adult Americans with (besides headaches) liberating proof that it is possible to have a good time while disdaining conventional symbols.

So many of the game's players, as well as its symbols, have changed. Many Americans have lost interest in status showing off, as is handily deduced from a *Wall Street Journal* headline of this very season: MOST BOSSES SHUN SYMBOLS OF STATUS. Other Americans have taken to picking their symbols to reflect values other than social rank. In *The New Elite*, out this year, David Lebedoff reports that professional and artistic Americans have begun shrugging aside the traditional symbols of economic rank. Says Lebedoff: "They can't afford them, so they downplay them. A mink coat at a faculty party is a disaster." Another social critic, John Brooks, suggests (in *Showing Off in America; From Conspicuous Consumption to Parody Display*) that people are undermining the traditional status competition by mocking it. Says Brooks, for instance, of those who sport so-called high-tech décor in their homes: "They flaunt commercial and industrial objects to prove that they don't have to be serious about such matters."

The confusion of the U.S. status race has been abetted by, among all else, the widespread adulteration of the very idea of the status symbol. The phrase has long since been stretched into an all-purpose label that gets promiscuously stuck on things that symbolize not status but mere fashion and faddishness. Even those graffiti-stamped T shirts that have had such a long, hot run of popularity have been called status symbols. Nonsense. If such garments symbolize status, it is surely the entire spectrum of status, high and low; the same can be said for those ubiquitous sports shirts with little alligators on the chest.

Careless use of the phrase tells just how frequently the meaning of status is overlooked by ostensible status auditors. Status is not merely rank, but rank within a hierarchy of esteem or prestige. The accouterments of style and fashion do not always or even usually amount to symbols of status. A privately owned yacht still symbolizes high financial status, but Sperry Top Siders—now worn by landlubbers of all varieties—no longer symbolize the status of yachtsman as they once did. Initialed handbags of the Louis Vuitton sort signaled uppering status in the days when people spoke of "going abroad"; now such bags have been so replicated that they represent little but the exhaustion of pop imagery. A VW Rabbit driven by a rich man dramatizes not status but conservation chic, in the same way that the now popular pickup truck, in the hands of suburbanites, is a symbol not of rank but of utilitarian chic. Some observers speak of solar heating panels as the new status symbols, but these devices do not dramatize social standing nearly as much as a philosophic (and economic) attitude. Those beepers that summon people to unseen telephones? Years ago, when they were rare, beepers emanated some prestige, but today, in profusion, they signal little but duty.

The status show, old style, still trudges on, to be sure, but it is most noticeable nowadays among the rich and most amusing to notice in Washington, which displays in concentration the social mode that reflects the country's ascendant mood. Says Diana McClellan, who closely monitors the status chase as the Washington *Post* gossip columnist: "There's more of a polarization now between the really rich and everybody else. These people are plastered with rubies and things to the point where you don't think you've got a chance. How can you hope to top $700,000 worth of Bulgari jewels around somebody's neck? You don't—you give up and go with plastic Scottie dogs or something."

Status, as notion or fact, is inseparable from the human condition. Given the nature of the U.S. as an open society cherishing the premise that anybody is free to rise, a good deal of status chasing was inescapable from the outset. If the chase had indeed rigidified the lines of class in the society, the symbols of status could only have become ever more clear. Reflecting upon that fact, one contemplates the present symbolic (and hierarchical) muddle with a light heart.

—*TIME*, December 21, 1981

The Game Of The Name

1978

"Giving a name," Thomas Carlyle once said, "is a poetic art." Perhaps, but it can also be a trying one. *Item:* Retreating before the distemper of feminists who do not like all hurricanes to bear women's names, Government meteorologists this year will christen storms not only Aletta but Bud and Daniel and Fico. *Item:* A national chain, Sambo's Restaurants, has run into stern resistance in New England, where civil rights groups are trying to ban the name because of allegedly racist overtones. *Item:* A young man who asked a Minnesota court to change his name to "1069" was recently refused and rebuked by the judge for proposing "an offense to human dignity" and seeking a name that was "inherently totalitarian." Strong language.

Strong feelings and forensics to match are commonplace when names are at stake—and they seem to be at stake all the time and all over the place in the U.S. The necessity of naming 3 million babies a year is only one source of nameless stress. Americans continually leap into flaps and furors over the naming and renaming of things and places. It amounts to a national obsession, or craze, or fascination, or mania—name it what you will—and it seems to be getting livelier all the time.

The name game is also growing ever more trendy and even desperate as more and more people clamor for attention in a please-notice-me society. It is merely ironic that businesses with names like the No Name Bar and The Chocolate Soup (a children's clothes store) now so proliferate that only an innocent would suffer a double take on learning that an orchestra called The Widespread Depression happened to be performing last week at a nightspot called The Other End. That is in Greenwich Village, where some runners trade at a store called The Athlete's Foot.

It is not easy to diagnose such nominal absurdity, but plainly it is epidemic. Already the name thing has inspired the publication of whole books that purport to plumb the "psychological vibrations" of personal names. Dawn and Loretta and Candy are supposed to be sexy, according to Christopher Andersen's *The Name Game,* and Bart and Mac and Nate are macho. Humphrey is sedentary; so much for Bogart. Anyway Americans have not needed any tracts or theories to get them lunging after catchy handles. One Phoenix mother recently branded her new baby girl with the unforgettable sobriquet Equal Rights Amendment.

The game is ubiquitous. Corporations strain to invent short, arcane names. Married women have begun to resist taking their husbands' surnames. Cassius Clay becomes Muhammad Ali in mid-career. Sambo is a target of only one minority; Italians hate the name Mafia. Rock groups, such as Jefferson Starship (*né* Airplane) and the Grateful Dead, have stretched the art of naming to surreal heights and depths. The President's wish to stick to Jimmy as his official name perhaps ingratiated him more with the public than any other step he has taken—and may, in the end, have hinted more than he intended at his fuzzy grasp of presidential power.

But what, in the name of heaven, is behind so much fuss over a matter as superficial as names—mere words, mere sounds, mere labels? Names are loved and hated as though they were animate. Kids may still be taught that only sticks and stones break bones, but grownups behave as though names are powerful agents for good or ill. In the adult world, name-calling is considered the dirtiest form of fight. Elaborate libel laws rest on the premise that a name can do real damage. Individuals clearly expect a variety of benefits when they take on new names. For Ellen Cooperman, becoming Ellen Cooperperson was ostensibly indispensable to her liberation. When he planned to run for Governor, Maryland Attorney General Francis Boucher Burch, long called "Bill," legally adopted the nickname with its suggestion of a common touch—but reverted to Francis Boucher after he withdrew from the race. Out of a simple wish to escape the paternal shadow, Graham Williams Wheeler, the son of Kansas City, Missouri, Mayor Charles B. Wheeler Jr., recently had his name legally pruned back to Graham Williams.

Even impersonal names stir improbable emotions. Phone clients have continued to howl as Ma Bell has systematically abolished exchange names (Butterfield, Murray Hill) in favor of numbers. When a disease got named for their organization, some American Legionnaires protested as though fearing voodoo-like contamination. Real estate developers act as if they expect fanciful street names to impart class to entire neighborhoods. But should it be assumed that only classical music is played on Symphony Circle in Vienna, Virginia?

People act, in short, as though names do possess strange power. Indeed, some names act as though they have the upper hand, sometimes persisting against all efforts at eradication. Cape Canaveral stuck where it was put long ago in spite of efforts to displace it with the chimerical name of Kennedy. Sixth Avenue remains just that to many New Yorkers in spite of diligent efforts to promote the general use of the 33-year-old legal name, Avenue of the Americas. Mount McKinley is still not generally accepted by Alaskans, who tend to prefer the peak's original designation, Denali.

Such cases suggest that a name is not a passive label. Some names, weirdly enough, manage to penetrate to the core of the named, achieving a profound fusion, becoming inextricable. Certain names become so incorporated with the acts or traits or destinies of their owners that they pop into the popular vocabulary as common nouns and adjectives: Cain, Jeremiah, Job (the Bible is a storehouse of such), Machiavelli, De Sade, McCarthy. The same peculiar joining of character and name occurs all the time, even in the fictive world. Romeo is as inseparable from the youth so named as he was from Juliet, and no actress could credibly play the role of Desdemona if the character's name were changed to, say, Sally. Some names veritably become the named, or vice versa—which is why everybody so naturally speaks of celebrated persons as "big names."

Many snatches of American vernacular rise out of an implied belief in the mystical properties of names. To say that someone's "name is mud" is figuratively to eradicate the owner. An American speaking of the crux or essence of any pursuit will probably say "That's the name of the game." Obviously, James Russell Lowell was onto something when he wrote that "there is more force in names than most men dream of..."

People in earlier civilizations and some primitive tribes up to modern times did dream—and believe—that personal names held mortal power. In *The Golden Bough*, Sir James Frazer tells how the ancient Egyptians and aboriginal Australians alike took pains to protect their secret true names—and the vital power they contained—from falling into the possession of outsiders. Aging Eskimos, Frazer also records, sometimes take new names in the belief they thus get a fresh start in life. Such superstitions have waned in today's civilizations. Still, as Noah Jacobs points out in *Naming-Day in Eden*, people "have not altogether discarded the belief in the virtue of names."

Actually, the potency of names is recognized more clearly and used more craftily than ever in this age of advertising. Name recognition is accepted as vital by both politicians and businesses. Ohio's ex-Congressman Wayne Hays, unsavory reputation and all, recently won a state legislative primary largely because of name recognition. Companies now calling themselves Equifax and Standex want to plant themselves in the public mind, while signaling that they are in tune with the technotronic times. And hucksters have long relied on the power of a clever name to sway a customer's decision. The popularity of Cheer and All among detergents, and Mustang and Diplomat among autos is no more due to the properties of the merchandise than the box-office power of a John Wayne movie is usually owed to artistic excellence. The hottest new perfume, now U.S.-bound from Paris, is called Opium. No telling how the doomed Edsel might have done if it had been dubbed, say, the Frolic.

The name game, though epidemic, will probably do no serious harm unless it at last hypnotizes everybody into forgetting that substance remains vitally important. Already far too many things that reach the American market under beguiling names turn out, on close inspection, to be turkeys and lemons.

—TIME, August 14, 1978

TIME TO REFLECT ON BLAH-BLAH-BLAH

1980

Late in his career, Announcer Bill Stern made an endearing confession about his vocal ways as the Christopher Columbus of television sportscasting. Said he: "I had no idea when to keep my big, fat, flapping mouth shut." The insight dawned too late to be of much use to Stern, but it might have been of value as a guide for his heirs. Unfortunately, nobody in the broadcast booth was listening. The result is the TV sports event as it is today: an entertainment genre in which an athletic game must compete for attention with the convulsive concatenations of blah-blah-blah that passes for commentary.

Television sportscasters, in short, are still a long way from mastering the art of the zipped lip. It is this familiar fact that has legions of sports fans eagerly looking forward to a special telecast of a football game that NBC has promised for Saturday, Dec. 20. The teams and site (Jets *vs.* Dolphins at Miami) are of little importance compared with the radical innovation that will be the main attraction: the absence of the usual game commentary. Thus the telecast will offer—and here Sports Columnist Red Smith leads the cheers— "no banalities, no pseudo-expert profundities phrased in coachly patois, no giggles, no inside jokes, no second-guessing, no numbing prattle." Just one announcer will be on hand, says NBC, to offer only the sort of essential information (injuries, rulings) that a stadium announcer traditionally provides. The prospect is engaging, even if it may be shocking to see a game presented merely for the sake of the drama on the field.

This blabber-proof telecast looms as far too rare an occasion to waste only in joy over a trial separation from the stream of half-consciousness that usually accompanies athletic endeavors on the tube. While sports fans will surely relish the moment, it should also be seized for grander purposes, for awareness may just be dawning in the Age of Communication that silence is indeed often golden. President-elect Ronald Reagan has so far, often to the chagrin of the press, shown an admirable reluctance to grab all of the many chances he gets to sound off on just about anything. Given the possible alternatives, Yoko Ono's fiat that John Lennon's passing be marked with ten minutes of silence around the world was inspired. In truth, the day of the telecast experiment would be a perfect time for the nation to reflect generally—and silently—on the whole disgruntling phenomenon of superfluous talk.

The American tendency to unchecked garrulity is most conspicuous in the realm of TV sports, but it does not begin or end there by a long shout. The late-evening TV news, for example, is aclutter with immaterial chatter. "Hap-py talk, keep talkin' hap-py talk . . ." Rodgers and Hammerstein offered that lyrical advice to young lovers, but a great many TV news staffers have adopted it as an inviolable rule of tongue. Hap-py talk is not reprehensible, but should it be force-fed to an audience looking for the news? Surely not, no more than a sports fancier tuning in football should be obliged to endure Tom Brookshier and Pat Summerall happily going over their personal travel schedules.

Admittedly, there is not likely to be universal agreement on precisely what talk is superfluous when. The judgment is aesthetic, and tastes vary. Some Americans might regard all sermons, lectures and political speeches as superfluous. Such testiness, however, can be shrugged off as a symptom of hyperactive intelligence. The criteria for talk should be appropriateness and pertinency. The essential question is: Does it subtract from or enhance the moment into which it falls? The deeper reason that sports commentary is annoying is that it so often ruptures the flow of the main event. The effect is easier to see when one imagines it occurring in the middle of a true drama, *Othello*, say:

"Now here's the video tape again with still another angle on Iago as he evilly fingers Desdemona's hanky. And look! Iago is curling the old lip just a trifle. Nice curl too, eh, Chuck? This chap was learning lip curling when the rest of that cast couldn't find the proscenium arch with both hands. Incidentally, about that hanky—you know, the star himself bought that hanky for 79¢ at Lamston's just before opening when it turned out the prop man used the real thing as a dustcloth. Now back to the action onstage..."

Existence today often means escaping from the latest Oscar award acceptance speech only to be trapped within earshot of a disc jockey who considers it a felony to fall silent for a second. Some 5,000 radio and TV talk shows fill the air with an oceanic surf of gabble, a big fraction of it as disposable as a weather-caster's strained charm. It is easy to snap off and tune out, but it is not so simple to elude real-life blather. Try to get away from it all, and soon a stage-struck airline captain will be monologuing about terrain miles below and half-obscured by the cloud cover. Go to the dentist, and the procedure is all but ordained: thumbs fill the mouth, the drill starts to whine, and a voice begins to express all those unpalatable political opinions.

At the movies, it is usually the couple two rows back who turn out to be practitioners of voice-over chic, tenderly broadcasting all the half-baked thoughts they ever half-understood about Fellini. Dial a phone number and the absent owner's talking machine coughs a set piece of cuteness before granting a moment for you to interject a brief message. As for bridge players, the typical foursome hardly finishes the play of a hand before the air burbles with a redundant rehashing of it all.

Personality, roles and situations all work in the chemistry that induces excessive chatter. And certain subjects pull the stopper on even temperate people. Food, for example, instigates a preposterous quantity of repetitious chat. Sex? It has already provoked such an excess of discussion—functional and gynecological—that it is fair to rule all future comment on the subject may be surplus.

Cabbies and barbers have long been assailed for marathon talking, but it is unjust that they so often wind up at the top of the list of nuisances. Indeed, cabbies are often mute and sullen, and ever since barbers became stylists they have felt sufficiently superior to clients that their urge to talk has diminished.

To be nettled by untimely yakking does not imply the advocacy of universal silence. A rigorous discipline, silence is practiced by certain monks and others who believe that it heightens the soul's capacity to approach God. For ordinary people, a bit of silence may occasionally seem golden, but what they mostly need is the conversation that keeps them close to others. Those who do not get enough talk tend to wither in spirit.

Says Linguistics Scholar Peter Farb in *Word Play*: "Something happened in evolution to create Man the Talker." And a talker man remains, with speech his most exalting faculty. Talk is the tool, the toy, the comfort and joy of the human species. The pity is that talkers so often blurt so far beyond the line of what is needed and desired that they have to be listened to with a stiff upper lip.

—*TIME*, December 22, 1980

So You Want To Be A Journalist

1974

Dear Nephew:

Congratulations on your decision to become a journalist, also on your healthy wish to get familiar with what's available before you set your course. Journalism is a growth industry, of course, diverse and getting more so all the time. I'll do my best to acquaint you with the whole picture as time goes by. For a start you ought to browse over the primary categories of the trade with some attention to their primary purposes and see if anything grabs you. Some of these are:

New Journalism, whose main purpose is the vivid display of the psyche, wit, charm, cunning and ruthlessness of the practitioner, as well as of that superb lighter-than-air quality the New Journalist obtains by his peculiar liberation from the laws of gravity, evidence and causality.

Broadcast Journalism, whose main purpose can be distinguished from that of Show Business only by the immaculate rule that deprives serious commentators of the freedom to emote over atrocities while granting it to disc jockeys and Sammy Davis, Jr.

Wire Service Journalism, whose main purpose is the compulsive accumulation of facts which it is prohibited by ancient dogma from arranging in any way that might hint or imply that facts arise out of human conditions subject to comprehension.

Newsmagazine Journalism, whose main purpose is the design, engineering and construction of dramatic parables upon which facts not astonishingly different from the wire services' can be arrayed like baubles on a Christmas tree for the enjoyment of the whole family.

Underground Journalism, whose main purpose is the prolongation of intellectual puberty for a stable of readers presumably doomed to suffer forever the appetite for gamy graffiti that has been assuaged by age eleven in anybody fortunate enough to grow up where sidewalks are clean enough to be chalked on.

Tape-Recorder Journalism, whose main purpose is to preserve for posterity encyclopedic quantities of direct quotations from people whose conversational life always seems to have peaked at the moment they have said, "Pass the salt, please."

Interpretative Journalism, whose main purpose is to absolve the electorate (and journalism) of all blame after it has honored some scoundrel, brigand, blackguard, thief or ignoramus with high office by exercising extrasensory perceptions that prove neither the voters (nor journalists) had any cause to suppose that the honoree would not be instantly cured of his life-long flaws by the healing powers of the oath of office.

Glossy Journalism, whose main purpose is the entirely humane one of assisting in the simulation of *actual life* by models, starlets, athletes, lottery winners and beautiful people whose destiny or fate is to have come to the attention of some editor desperately needing 112 lines of type to fill in the space between the Drambuie and Tampax ads.

Cultural Journalism, whose main purpose is to cut the hearts out of working artists and thus prepare their bodies for use as a platform upon which the Cultural Journalist performs precious little tap-dances that incite other Cultural Journalists to coo, salivate and chirp erudite witticisms while wolfing peanuts and colleagues at cultural freeloads.

Financial Journalism, whose main purpose is to keep alive an ancient technique of legerdemain through which the Financial Journalist is enabled to relieve himself in a reader's ear while utterly convincing him it is actually raining outside.

Pundit Journalism, whose main purpose is to provide busy work and pasturage for resonant and well-connected journalists who have outgrown toil, prevalent realities and teachability, and who thus go forth touchingly unaware that Adam Smith is dead, that elections have no bearing on events, that the Government doesn't govern, and that, no, Congress is not going to take a look at the Military Industrial Complex next year either.

Advocacy Journalism, whose main purpose is to convince the innocent and gullible that the Mafia will act nicer if only a Presbyterian is elected Godfather.

Liberation Journalism, whose main purpose is to arouse loathing for the white-male-straight culture into the rotten thick of which it hopes to facilitate the passage of certain citizens who have been rendered idiosyncratic and underprivileged by virtue of their gender, coloration or grazing habits.

Gonzo Journalism, whose main purpose is to provide occupational therapy for any writer who has inadvertently collided with an event while advertently colliding with seven uppers, three downers, four six-packs, a fifth, a Great Speckled Bird and a meat-ball wedge.

Play Ball Journalism, whose main purpose is to service young executives who can't risk having a copy of *Screw* found in the old attache case by providing them the same fare cunningly camouflaged as marshmallow-topped Ovaltine whose nutritional value is validated from time to time by female psychologists who not only don't mind carrying Screw in an attache case but keep it on the coffee table right alongside the *Mental Hygiene Quarterly*.

With-It Journalism, whose main purpose is to provide a continual fresh supply of stunning celebrity journalists whose names can be rented for use as bait by dedicated entrepreneurs when they go reverently begging money from establishment banks to finance irreverent With-It Journals.

Hot-Brain Journalism, whose body, to the extent that it has one, exists primarily in New York City, and whose main purpose (as cousin Harry Ashmore observed long ago in only slightly different words) is to dazzle an audience consisting almost entirely of itself with prodigious pyrotechnics that brilliantly light up the sky with no risk whatever of illuminating the landscape below.

Well, son, that's enough for starters. You mull it over. I realize you wanted to hear something about my own field, but, frankly, even though it has brought me an almost indecent amount of fun, I can't imagine a young man being interested. I am engaged in what you might call Out-of-It Journalism. Its main and in fact only purpose is to let people know *what's up*. I'd be surprised if you found this very attractive once you are aware of all the other opportunities available.

—MORE, February, 1974

FOUR

A Few Symbol-Minded Questions

Why So Much Is Beyond Words

Slogan Power! Slogan Power!

Looking For Mr. President

The Trivial State Of The States

States' Rights And Other Myths

The Public Life Of Secrecy

Why Doesn't My Government Stop Lying To Me?

The Busting Of American Trust

A Few Symbol-Minded Questions

1989

Lawmakers looking for a way to protect the flag have a lot of searching to do if they hope to cover all possibilities. An amendment or statute simply outlawing desecration of the U.S. flag is not going to do the job. Potential loopholes and tricky questions abound. For instance:

If there is only one official U.S. flag, would it be permissible to burn an unofficial one—say, an obsolete model with 48 stars? Since a flag is, by usual definition, made of fabric, should a wooden representation of it be protected? What about little lapel pins or cuff links with flags on them? What if somebody publicly stomped a piece of such jewelry?

By custom, the U.S. flag is often called "the red, white and blue." Should the nation prohibit the abuse of any red-white-and-blue decoration? Should it be a crime to burn red-white-and-blue bunting? Or foreign flags of red, white and blue? Incidentally, should "the red, white and blue" be considered a flag when represented in black and white?

What if somebody burned one of those decorative wind socks that are fashioned with a blue field of white stars and red and white stripes to suggest the U.S. flag? A crime?

What if vulgar protesters wiped the ground with a flag designed exactly like the U.S. flag—but colored orange, brown and green? Should that be an offense? Should making such a flag equal desecration?

Should a law protecting the flag also protect homemade facsimiles of the flag? Is a crayon drawing of the flag a flag?

Besides burning, what would constitute the "physical" desecration some of our political leaders emphasize they hope to outlaw? Does that include obscenely wagging a finger at a flag? Sticking out one's tongue at the flag? Thumbing a nose at the flag? What if some miscreant mooned the flag? Or stuck pins in the flag—in public?

At present, burning the President in effigy is lawful. Should it be unlawful to burn an effigy of the flag? Is the flag more important than the President?

Indeed, is the flag more important than any other American symbol? Or should the statute or amendment be expanded to protect all significant national symbols? What if protesters burned a model of the White House? Should that be a crime?

Suppose the national anthem got desecrated? What if somebody deliberately sang or played it off-key? What if a dissident publicly stomped a tinkling music box while it was playing *The Star-Spangled Banner*? Should that be allowed?

If flag burning is outlawed, should it still be all right to burn the U.S. Constitution? Or the Declaration of Independence? Or (gasp!) the *Congressional Record*?

Is the flag even more important than Congress? Imagine that protesters burned the entire U.S. Congress in effigy. Would that be O.K.? What if each tiny effigy were wearing a teensy-weensy lapel flag?

Should states be permitted to electrocute a condemned prisoner with a flag tattooed on his chest? Should burning the flag be a more serious crime than burning a church? More serious than burning a cross?

Should the nation permit postage stamps bearing pictures of the flag to be defaced by inky cancellations?

Commercial exploitation of the flag is commonplace in print, on television and around business premises. Since such use (almost by definition) debases the flag, should it be outlawed? What should be done about garments featuring a flaglike motif? When a flag is cut and sewed into a shirt, is it still a flag?

Does political exploitation debase the flag? Should it be prohibited?

Philosophically speaking, is it even possible to desecrate the U.S. flag? One can desecrate something that is sacred, holy or religious (which is just what desecrate primarily means, according to the *Oxford English Dictionary*). Is the U.S. flag sacred, holy or religious? Or is it a symbol of a secular state?

If the flag is now a secular symbol, would an amendment against desecrating it, transform it, by implication, into a sacred symbol? Would such an act approximate the founding of a state religion?

If the flag is a sacred, holy or religious symbol, is the worship of it idolatry? Would a flag-worshiping congregation be exempt from taxes like other churches? Should flag burning be considered desecration even if the burner does not believe it to be sacred, holy or religious? Does sacredness exist in a physical object or in the mind of the object's worshiper? There seems no end to such questions.

Answers are not as plentiful. It is not enough to say, as a New York State senator once said, "We want people to respect the flag, and if they will not respect it voluntarily, then we will make them respect it involuntarily." Toward that end, lawmakers might get useful guidance from the Alien and Sedition Acts. Passed in 1798, they were enforced in a way that made a crime of any idea, opinion, remark or act a judge disapproved of. One New Jersey man was arrested and fined $100 for saying he did not care if somebody fired a cannon up the President's arse.

Funny, the laws that made it sedition to speak ill of the President and the Government contained no provision against flag desecration. Still, Federalist judges sitting at the time would have been happy to imprison any Jeffersonian Republican who abused the flag. Among the Americans the Federalists did put behind bars was the author of a placard that urged NO STAMP ACT, NO SEDITION AND NO ALIEN ACTS.

And newspapers sternly denounced as "seditious" a group that burned not the flag, but the Alien and Sedition Acts.

That raises yet another question: Should it be a crime to burn a statute or constitutional amendment that makes flag burning a crime?

—*TIME,* August 28, 1989

WHY SO MUCH IS BEYOND WORDS

1981

"In the beginning," says the Gospel of St. John, "was the Word." The mystical meanings that the Bible lays upon the word Word are not embraced by everyone. Yet nobody can reasonably doubt that the coming of the word, if not the Word, to humankind was the start of something big in history. Human talk may have struck dyspeptic Nathaniel Hawthorne like "the croak and cackle of fowls," but the rise of language, written and spoken, is all but universally rated as one of the glories of the species. What is surprising is that in the common give and take of daily living people still rely so little upon the verbal language that distinguishes them from the beasts.

In fact, Homo sapiens, as a communicator, does not seem to have come all that far from the time when grunts and gesticulations were the main ways of getting messages across. Both individuals and groups still send vital messages by gesture, by pantomime, by dramatics—by a dizzy diversity of what scholars call nonverbal communication. The reality is easy to overlook in an epoch that is bloated with pride in its dazzling technical marvels of communication. Yet, in spite of human garrulousness, perhaps as little as 20% of the communication among people is verbal, according to experts; most, by far, even when talk is going on, consists of nonverbal signals.

This is true of men, women, children, individually and in groups of all sizes. Nations and the realm of politics lean heavily on indirect gesture and charades to convey important messages. Take Secretary of State Alexander Haig's talks in China: Was not his actual purpose to send a signal to the Soviets? Societies signal prevalent values to their members by what is applauded and what condemned; status symbol is synonymous with status signal. "Language," said Samuel Johnson, "is the dress of thought." But all over the world people act as though language were mere costume—and usually a disguise. Everybody (evidently nobody can help it) tends to mimic that anonymous signaler cited in *Proverbs:* "He winketh with his eyes, he speaketh with his feet, he teacheth with his fingers."

This tendency to commune by semaphore has probably not increased at all in centuries, but consciousness of it surely has. A spate of books like this season's *Reading Faces* and last decade's popular *Body Language* have explored the individual's tendency to broadcast things (unconsciously and otherwise) through all manner of physical movement and facial gymnastics. Such matters, made widely familiar by pop sociology, anthropology and psychology, have become the stuff of common conversation. Michael Korda's *Power! How to Get It, How to Use It,* like other books of this ilk, is mainly a primer in how to manipulate others by a cold-blooded control of nonverbal signals that occur commonly in the workaday world: for example, how executives signal their style and presumptions of power by the clothes they choose and the way they arrange their office furniture.

At work or play, everybody emits wordless signals of infinite variety. Overt, like a warm smile. Spontaneous, like a raised eyebrow. Involuntary, like leaning away from a salesperson to resist a deal. Says Julius Fast in *Body Language:* "We rub our noses for puzzlement. We clasp our arms to isolate ourselves or to protect ourselves. We shrug our shoulders for indifference." Baseball pitchers often dust back a batter with a close ball that is not intended to hit but only to signal a warning claim of dominance. The twitchings of young children too long in adult company are merely involuntary signals of short-fused patience. Any competent psychiatrist remains alert to the tics and quirky expressions by which a patient's hidden emotions make themselves known. People even signal by the odors they give off, as Janet Hopson documents in superfluous detail in *Scent Signals: The Silent Language of Sex*. Actually, it is impossible for an individual to avoid signaling other people; the person who mutely withdraws from human intercourse sends out an unmistakable signal in the form of utter silence.

Sociologist Dane Archer calls reading such signals "social intelligence," but the phrase's greatest usefulness was probably in completing the title of his book *How to Expand Your Social Intelligence Quotient*. Urged Archer: "We must unshackle ourselves from the tendency to ignore silent behavior and to prefer words over everything else." The evidence all over is that while people meander the earth through thickets of verbiage (theirs and others), many, perhaps most, do pay more attention to wordless signals and are more likely to be influenced and governed by nonverbal messages.

Nothing but the daily news is necessary to show the reliance that rulers and nations place upon nonverbal communication. Presidents soon learn that they can hardly do anything that is not taken to be a signal of some sort to somebody. So it is, too, with the governments under them. In March President Reagan, questioned about lifting the post-Afghanistan embargo on grain sales to the U.S.S.R., told reporters that he did not see how he could do it "without sending the wrong signal"—which is exactly what critics accused him of when he did kill the embargo the next month. Why did the Senate Foreign Relations Committee reject Ernest Lefever as the nation's top human rights official? Partly because of a fear that other countries might construe support of Lefever as a signal of national sympathy for his unenthusiastic attitude toward a strong American human rights policy. Why do some defense strategists support building the MX missile at a cost of about $40 billion? Not entirely because of its possible military efficacy, but also because of what a commitment to such a system might signal the Soviet Union about U.S. resolve.

The bloody history of the world ought to be the first item of evidence in any case against relying on wordless signaling in international affairs. The opportunities for misunderstanding are immense and constant. Says Harvard Law Professor Roger Fisher, a specialist in international negotiations: "The chances of properly understanding signals in the midst of conflict is always very slight." For instance, during the Iran hostage negotiations, Secretary of State Cyrus Vance, intending to signal the belief that U.S.-Iran problems could be resolved, spoke of restoring "normal" diplomatic relations. Iran mistakenly took that to mean a return to things as they were under the despised Shah. Says Fisher: "Sending diplomatic signals is like sending smoke signals in a high wind."

As all but the very luckiest—or dullest—of people might testify, individual signals have a way of misfiring just as easily, with results just as calamitous if not as earthshaking. The danger of misunderstanding increases dramatically when even the most elementary signals are used by people in different cultures. The happiest of overt American signals, the circled thumb and index finger, unless accompanied by a smile, amounts to an insult in France. The innocent American habit of propping a foot on a table or crossing a leg in figure-four style could cause hard feelings among Arabs, to whom the showing of a shoe sole is offensive.

People indulge in nonverbal communication not basically to be clever or devious but because these ways of communicating are deeply embedded in the habits of the species and automatically transmitted by all cultures. So says Anthropologist Ray Birdwhistell, a pioneer in the study of kinesics, as body language is called. Other experts point out that signaling by movement occurred among lizards and birds, as well as other creatures, even before mammals emerged.

Unfortunately, no useful dictionary of gestures is really possible, since every gesture and nonverbal expression depends for meaning on the variants of both the individual using it and the culture in which it takes place. Says Anthropologist Edward T. Hall, author of *The Silent Language and Beyond Culture:* "Because of its complexity, efforts to isolate out 'bits' of nonverbal communication and generalize from them in isolation are doomed to failure. Book titles such as *How to Read a Person Like a Book* are thoroughly misleading, doubly so because they are designed to satisfy the public's need for highly specific answers to complex questions for which there are no simple answers."

Sooner or later, for any word lover, the human habit of wordless signaling leads to a simple question for which there is perhaps only a complex answer. The question is why has language, given its unique power to convey thought or feeling or almost anything else in the human realm, fallen so short as a practical social tool for man. The answer is that it has not. Instead, the human creature has fallen short as a user of language, employing it so duplicitously that even in ancient times the wise advised that people should be judged not by what they said but by what they did. That such advice holds good for today goes, alas, without saying.

—*TIME,* July 13, 1981

Slogan Power! Slogan Power!

1979

The lusty cry that roused the Highlanders of ancient Scotland for battle was called a *sluagh-gairm*. A combination of the Gaelic words for host and cry, this rallying shout became *slogorne* in English and was over generations altered into *sluggorne, slughorn, slogurn* and other variants, including *slogen*. From that came the modern word that embraces those catch phrases, mottoes, aphorisms and partisan whoops that are continually coined and used by every segment of society, from politicians to Boy Scouts to terrorists. Slogans are, in fact, as common as chitchat.

The birth of the slogan itself, with whatever name, goes back to the start of history; as far back as human records occur, so do slogans. On the basis of its power alone, its potential capacity to unite people and move them toward either belligerent or peaceful goals, the slogan rates as one of man's most ingenious and economical verbal inventions. So the ubiquity of slogans in modern times is understandable, and it probably does more good than harm. Still, there is reason to wonder whether the use—and abuse—of slogans has not at last resulted in a period of fatigue, a sort of slump that might be called sloganosis.

Nothing has raised the question more forcefully than President Carter's embarrassing effort in his State of the Union speech to establish his Administration's slogan. Although his staff has had two years to mull over the matter, what they came up with was something called New Foundation. It foundered. Some people yawned; others were derisive. Mainly, everyone was magnificently uninspired. New Foundation just did not have the ring of the great slogans of yesteryear: New Deal, Fair Deal, New Frontier, Great Society. Still, the Carter dud was only a conspicuous example of the general anemia that has beset sloganeering in recent years. Some believe, for example, that the commercial practice of the art has fallen into something of a slump partially because advertising now gives so much attention to research-based claims that it has somewhat neglected the old stand-by.

For all that, sloganeering is far from going out of style. The slogan is, after all, probably the best people mover this side of earthquakes, court orders and guns. A first-rate slogan is potent indeed when properly contrived. It becomes as easy to remember as it is hard to forget. It plants itself in the consciousness by rhythm, rhyme, pith or brevity. Once there, it works not only by whatever imagery it carries but—more—by the latent emotions it mobilizes. It plays too on the verities and prejudices of its audience, balming or inflaming them according to purpose. Just so, the slogan lurks as a sort of floating hook in the psyche. Properly tugged, it can impel people to coalesce, to divide, to fight, to sacrifice, to vote, to buy.

Yet the power of rousing phrases was recognized long before anybody knew how or why it worked. Some equivalent of "Hail to the Chief" no doubt glued people to their governments from the moment tribes first formed, just as, later, did "Long live the King!" History has left a litter of slogans from all its great events, civil as well as martial—and not only political history. After Pope Urban II in 1095 called for war to recapture the Holy Land, the spontaneous outcry of listening clerics—"God wills it!"—helped fire up Christendom for the First Crusade. The translation of philosophy and doctrine into slogans has assisted in every major political turnabout, from Runnymede to Yalta. Indeed, the history of the U.S. can plausibly be capsuled in a litany of slogans: No taxation without representation. Give me liberty or give me death. Don't fire until you see the whites of their eyes. Let the people rule. Horace Greeley's popularization of "Go West, young man" not only helped inspire California-bound migration but even today conjures up appealing images. "Speak softly and carry a big stick" brings back the vanished world of Theodore Roosevelt's America. Modern America? The war to end war. A chicken in every pot. We have nothing to fear but fear itself. Remember Pearl Harbor. We shall overcome. Hell no, we won't go. Whip inflation now.

Today's slogans, too often unmemorable, still encode the directions in which people are trying to move their countrymen. Combatants in the abortion arena rally around "right to life" and "freedom of choice." Opponents of nuclear power cry, "No nukes," while proponents answer that it is "safer than sex." Liberated homosexuals chant, "Gay pride"; their detractors plead, "Save our children." Blacks employ "black is beautiful" for self-encouragement and "black power" as a statement to the established order. And the elderly now demand "gray power." Proposition 13, though a California event, has become a rallying call everywhere among rebels hoping to achieve tax reductions. The movie *Network* has given the country an all-purpose battle cry: "I'm mad as hell, and I'm not going to take it any more!"

The cream of the contemporary crop of slogans is still found in the creations of the advertising trade, which of course was the first to exploit psychology and behaviorism to turn the art of persuasion into a quasi-science. The success of its catchwords is confirmed by retail sales figures that make even the national deficit seem a trifle. More to the point, anyone can confirm the sticking power of business's best slogans simply by scavenging around in the mind: Does she or doesn't she? Even your best friends won't tell you. Ask the man who owns one. Say it with flowers. Up, up and away. Fly now, pay later. You're in safe hands. Plop, plop, fizz, fizz. Good to the last drop. The high-priced spread. Tastes good like a cigarette should. Leave the driving to us. I'd rather fight than switch. When it rains, it pours. We try harder. It floats. A diamond is forever.

Such a list could go on almost forever. This fact indeed suggests one possible explanation for the fatigue, or sloganosis, that diminishes the sparkle of the current slogan output. Could it be that we are witnessing a weird new form of inflation? Is it conceivable that just as an oversupply of money drives down the value of currency, an excess of sloganizing diminishes the catchiness of catchwords and the public's vulnerability to their magic? Who could dare say for sure? Yet the theory offers at least one hope of an eventual recovery.

There are those, of course, who would like to see sloganeering die off entirely. Precisely because the art appeals to emotion, some idealists and intellectual purists disdain it in favor of cool, rational discourse. This crowd is clearly trying to swim against a very strong human current. Moreover, they are out of touch with the problems of both leadership and the human dilemma. The problem has never been to get people to *think* about doing something. The difficulty has always been to get them to *act*. From time immemorial, leaders have found that one of the best ways, for good or ill, is to say, "Rally round the slogan, folks." It is not time for a change.

—*TIME*, February 12, 1979

LOOKING FOR MR. PRESIDENT

1979

Tall, stately John Connally of Texas "looks like a President." So wrote stocky, rumpled James Reston in the New York *Times* a couple of weeks ago. Since the assertion was right out of the Political Writer's Handy Kit of Solemn Banalities, it could be conscientiously forgotten. It probably will not be, so the question lingers: What does it mean?

The U.S. is eternally looking for somebody who supposedly looks like a President. Once again, the presidential field is prematurely swarming with contenders and pretenders, each selling a face and figure as heaven-sent for White House display. But how is one to judge? If the nation had a vivid idea of what *the* presidential look should be, political parties and voters alike would be saved considerable uncertainty.

Such a concept, alas, is not easy to come by. Political commentators have been more preoccupied with contrived presidential images than with actual looks. Some lofty thinkers even feel that the look of a President is of little significance. In reality, a leader's countenance and mien have always been of great moment to the led, and a President embodies an epic load of national symbolism. Externals have become ever more crucial since ubiquitous television has taken over as the main medium of campaigning. Today, as Daniel Boorstin notes in his book *The Image,* "our national politics has become a competition for images or between images, rather than between ideals."

If the founding fathers knew what a President should look like, they kept it to themselves. A President, says the Constitution, need only be a native-born resident and old enough (35) to be dry behind the ears. The law is mute on the shape and size of those ears and other elements of physiognomy, stature and hirsuteness that go into the chimerical mix of looks.

Most Americans have seen history take critical turns because of appearances. Thomas E. Dewey was hurt in both his campaigns for the White House because many voters agreed with snippy Alice Roosevelt Longworth that he looked "like the bridegroom on a wedding cake." In 1960 Richard Nixon's narrow loss to John Kennedy was greatly influenced by the scenes from that famous first televised debate. Nixon was recovering from a staph infection, and his gray visage was transmogrified into a haggard, glowering, shifty-eyed mask by the same cameras that broadcast a fresh, vigorous Kennedy. Nixon learned the lesson and in his second race, as Joe McGinniss documents in *The Selling of the President*, he paid much attention to such minutiae as makeup and stage gestures. Said the candidate to one TV cue man: "Now when you give me the 15-second cue, give it to me right under the camera. So I don't shift my eyes."

Still, who could say with certitude that Nixon did not look like a Chief Executive and that Kennedy did, or vice versa? Is a President clean-cut? Ulysses S. Grant would have fit right in at an Allen Ginsberg poetry reading. Trim? Honest Grover Cleveland's dreadnought corpulence might have served as a model for Thomas Nast's potbellied crooks. Is the presidential face august, humane, agleam with probity? John Adams might have been cast as Scrooge or a consecrated bookkeeper. John Quincy Adams looked incipiently satanic. James Monroe's bug-eyed visage might have got him followed by the FBI in the 1960s. Martin Van Buren's sweetly cunning countenance could have belonged to a real estate shark. William Henry Harrison looked bilious. Millard Fillmore at times resembled a triumph of dishevelment. William McKinley, says Edmund Morris in *The Rise of Theodore Roosevelt*, seemed the perfect picture of a President—but only "from the neck up." McKinley also owned stumpy legs, pulpy hands and a commanding gaze that was mobilized, says Morris, by a tormented effort "to concentrate a sluggish, wandering mind."

Physical peculiarities kept none of those gentlemen from the highest office, but some of them might have had a hard time getting there today. For Americans now even hold strong notions about the cut of a Chief Executive's clothes. Harry Truman incensed many button-down traditionalists by hacking around his Key West vacation retreat in criminally garish sports shirts. The spectacle of Franklin D. Roosevelt in the flamboyant cape and floppy hats that he loved to flaunt raised the blood pressure of old-school Republicans.

Granted the dizzying diversity of looks in the gallery of past Chief Executives, how is anyone to know what an ideal President should look like? The odd truth is that Americans *do* know. But how? What picture of a President resides in the popular imagination? What, in short, is the operating archetype?

It is not necessary to enter Carl Jung's collective unconscious and search among primordial archetypes (the great mother, the old man) that supposedly lurk there. It seems reasonable enough to suppose that Americans test the looks of would-be Presidents against an accumulating folkloric archetype, a fluid and ambiguous composite formed of several diverse figures.

What figures? They would be the handful of Presidents whose greatness is all but universally conceded. Mount Rushmore epically displays the main clutch of them—Washington, Jefferson, Lincoln, Teddy Roosevelt. A few more might be added—Jackson, Wilson, F.D.R. It is too soon to say which, if any, of the recent Presidents will ascend to the same folk pantheon. But the ghosts already there are quite likely astir in the elusive archetypal President.

Certainly, more than the faces and physiques of the greats have lent contours to the archetype. It is premature if not fatuous to say that any man looks like a President before he has done the job. Sixscore years ago, many voters thought that one candidate was much too awkward and homely to fit the task. He was, warts and all, Abraham Lincoln. Some time later, the majority of the electorate agreed that handsome, silver-haired, courtly Warren Harding looked every inch a President. His name lives still as a synonym for scandal and ineptitude. Ultimately, any President's face takes on mythic and symbolic significance only as a result of character—and deeds.

—*TIME*, April 9, 1979

THE TRIVIAL STATE OF THE STATES

1978

The envelope, please. And now, for the best performance by an American state legislature in the Much-Ado-About-Little category, the Golden Nit for 1978 goes to...

This is the homestretch of the silly season, when state legislatures across the land seem to vie for the imaginary Golden Nit. There is nothing imaginary, though, about the time, effort and deliberation they customarily devote to the trivial, the insignificant, the utterly negligible. Nebraska's legislature, for example, has just dealt with a bill to add, as consumer representatives, two corpses to the state anatomical board: that passes for humor in Lincoln. Rhode Island's senators breezily adopted a resolution praising the hairdo of a female legislator, but the house turned aside a proposal to decree ricotta the State Cheese. In Florida, the legislature recently indulged in boisterous repartee over a measure that would have made it a crime to molest the "skunk ape," a mythical critter occasionally sighted around the state that is said to stand 7 ft. tall, weigh 700 lbs. and smell like swamp gas.

This legislative preoccupation with the trivial, which is confirmed in almost every state capital, goes by the term microphilia. Though the ailment was named only a few years ago (by a justly obscure political diagnostician), it has been in evidence as long as state legislatures have existed—though sometimes upstaged by more dramatic defects such as procrastination, carelessness and venality. These larger historic faults were undoubtedly in the mind of John Burns when he wrote in *The Sometime Governments* (1970): "We expect very little of our legislatures, and they continually live up to our expectations." In fact, many state legislatures have improved in some respects over the past two decades, attracting members of higher caliber, for example, and tightening up their staffs and internal organization. But their fascination with trivia has, if anything, got worse; microphilia has become chronic and endemic in the statehouses.

In no area does this odd trait show itself as starkly as in the legislatures' ceaseless squabbling over the designation of "official" animals, birds, fishes, minerals, poems, songs and flowers. Last year, after interminable conflict among advocates of barbecue, gumbo and chili, Texas legislators finally designated the last as State Dish. This year a skirmish shaped up in the New York legislature over the selection of a State Insect (praying mantis *vs.* Karner blue butterfly), and in New Jersey over a State Fish (bluefish leading); a struggle over the wild turkey left Alabama still, alas, without a State Game Bird.

Vermont, in a flurry of accomplishment, designated a State Cold Water Fish (trout), a State Warm Water Fish (walleyed pike) and a State Insect (honey bee). The Massachusetts general court, though moving hardly at all on important issues, considered (and, amazingly, rejected) the adoption of a State Poem with the opening line, "Chickadee, chickadee, chickadee . . ." Connecticut, which got along for 190 years without a State Song, obtained one at last when the legislature picked *Yankee Doodle*—after replacing the word girls with folks. Widely criticized years ago for ending a session in which the designation of the Great Dane was its signal achievement, the Pennsylvania legislature this year bent its energies to the selection of a State Cat (alley cat favored). Success would create the possibility, as one statehouse joker put it, "of the State Dog chasing the State Cat up the State Tree [hemlock]."

Legislative microphilia ranges well beyond an obsession with official totems and artifacts. One classic manifestation occurred this season in Colorado, where legislators climaxed their session with a mighty struggle over the apostrophe in Pike's Peak: for the benefit of constituents who had never come to terms with grammar, they outlawed the apostrophe. In Alabama, legislators reached the session's final day without action on a single major bill—but not without having played, once again, their recurring conflict with the capital city government over parking space for their cars. Idaho lawmakers, for their part, indulged in a six-week-long brouhaha over whether to ban the use of radar by highway police; the senate passed a bill prohibiting it on the ground that radar endangers heart patients with pacemakers, and the house set aside the bill only after the sponsor admitted that there was absolutely no hard evidence of such a risk.

Resolutions of commendation, which pumped promiscuously out of most legislatures, got so overdone in South Carolina that one member this year exposed the absurdity with a resolution intended to commend "all persons, male and female, young and old, tall and short, fat and skinny, who have performed any act or deed during the past five months worthy of commendation." A sort of subdued microphilia was evident in Concord, where New Hampshire's solons spent several months intensely debating the question of whether they had any reason to be in session at all. In such an atmosphere it is not surprising that a typical legislative leader, New Jersey Assembly Speaker Christopher Jackman, could be recorded as telling his followers: "I don't want anyone asking me any questions and expecting me to give any answers."

When it takes a virulent turn, microphilia provokes that streak of rowdiness for which state legislatures have always been famous. Such episodes may not often match the one achieved some years ago in Austin, where Texas legislators

159

indulged in a fist-throwing free-for-all best remembered for the four lawmakers who occupied the rostrum and sang *I Had a Dream, Dear* while their colleagues slugged it out. And yet buffoonery such as the throwing of food (in Illinois) or of wastepaper (in Maryland) occurs frequently enough to show that the nation's microphiliacs have at best only a tenuous hold on dignity. In the Oklahoma house, members keep tiny American flags at hand to wave when the speaker happens to be Representative John Monks—who won fame of a sort for having once got an anticockfight bill killed by arguing that it was Communist-inspired. In Rhode Island this year a certain inordinate liveliness resulted when, on St. Patrick's Day, the members' water pitchers were filled with creme de menthe—as when, on the subsequent St. Joseph's Day, Italian members, countering the Irish, wore red hats and handed out pizza. In the Georgia legislature, decorum so deteriorated at one session that a member flung to the floor by an epileptic seizure got no immediate help because no one thought anything was wrong.

While the outcroppings of microphilia are plain to see, the cause of the condition is not so conspicuous. Actually, the legislative obsession with trivia is best understood in the same way a psychologist understands the compulsive quirks and tics of an individual—as a signal of unresolved inner frustrations. The main one of several unresolved twists in the legislative psyche is a baffled, often stifled, creative urge; thus action on trivia becomes a substitute for action on substantial matters. Viewed just so, microphilia can be seen as a symptom of the legislatures' historic and persisting aversion for using their powers, a trait, students of the species have long noted, that accounts for the fact that state government is the weakest link in the chain of American federalism. The same institutional frustration underlies many of the other dubious but widespread legislative characteristics that have put state legislatures right where University of

Pittsburgh Professor William Keefe once located them: "On the outskirts of public esteem and affection."

Only a grouch would regard all legislative levity with a solemn eye. Yet it is fair to marvel that these grass-roots lawmakers manage to do so much that is scarcely worth doing while assiduously avoiding so much that cries out to be done. Undoubtedly there are quite a few among the lawmakers themselves who may feel as Senator Jim Walters did when his Mississippi legislature went home this spring. The session's highlight, said he, was "that we didn't do any more damage to the people than we did."

Perhaps even that deserves thanksgiving. Surely by now Americans are accustomed to being grateful for any favors—however small—from the statehouse.

—*TIME*, May 29, 1978

STATES' RIGHTS AND OTHER MYTHS

1981

"It is my intention . . . to demand recognition of the distinction between the powers granted to the Federal Government and those reserved to the states or to the people."
—President Ronald Reagan,
Inaugural Address

Controversy over the distribution of American political power is older than the nation. The argument broke out as soon as Americans began thinking about uniting their states, and it has not stopped since. The dispute about what power lodged where grew fierce enough in the 19th century to explode into the Civil War, after which the notion of state sovereignty existed only as fantasy. Yet the issue remained flammable enough in modern times to bring on several grave federal-state confrontations, including a bloody one in the case of the desegregation of the University of Mississippi in 1962.

The fuss is apparently going to last forever. Fortunately, it does sometimes fizzle down to a pleasantly inaudible buzz. In fact, the country has enjoyed just such a lull in the years since Southern politicians stopped exhuming John Calhoun's interposition doctrine to resist desegregation. But now the lull is over. The oldest free-floating political issue in U.S. history is flaring up again, fueled by accumulated resentment at that familiar, all-purpose ogre: the huge, cumbersome, inefficient, ever busy Federal Government.

Concern about the workings and directions of the federal system has been climbing sharply and growing more articulate for the past few years, and not only among conservatives.

Says one self-styled "committed liberal and unapologetic Democrat," Arizona's Governor Bruce Babbitt: "The federal system is in complete disarray." The National Governors' Association last summer unanimously demanded that Congress and the President create a commission to diagnose the whole governmental apparatus and propose some sorting out of powers. An equally urgent plea for a realignment of powers came last summer from the Advisory Commission on Intergovernmental Relations, whose members include Congressmen, Governors, state legislators, mayors, county officials and private citizens.

Given a sympathetic new President with a keen interest in the subject, this impressive chorus of discontent will probably inspire the appointment of study commissions and the production of all kinds of reports, analyses and perhaps even proposals for change. But what action is apt to occur? Is any important rearrangement of the powers of federal and state governments likely? The prevailing suspicion is voiced by Michigan's Republican Lieutenant Governor James Brickley: "I'm not confident that anything substantial can be done."

Such caution is not necessarily cynical. It is common to anyone who keeps an eye on the realities of American government, as contrasted with the sentimental and doctrinaire preachings about it. One reality of political America is the country's capacity and willingness to do whatever is deemed practically or morally essential—while inventing the justifying doctrine as needed. The nation, operating under one Constitution, has permitted racial segregation in one era but outlawed it in another, tolerated corporate trusts in one season but tabooed them in a later, let the states oversee political parties at one time and taken them under the federal wing in another. One flaw of the usual federal-state debate is that participants often overlook the ad hoc evolution of the U.S. scheme of governance: they imagine that governmental structures take their shape more from the niceties of theory than from the proddings of a society beset with messy problems. As former Governor Orville Freeman of Minnesota once said: "The literature of federal-state relationships is replete with myths that need to be demolished."

While the tangled problems of today's governments are far from mythical, the dialogue over realigning powers will predictably be shot through with mythology. Once again, the states' rights catch phrase is being heard. But the Constitution assigns *rights* only to individuals, none to the states, which are granted only residual *powers* by the Tenth Amendment. It is argued that the Federal Government has left the states bereft of revenues. In fact, state taxing powers are limited only by their own constitutions, and presumably with popular approval.

An ever popular myth is that there once was, and might be again, a nice, neat division of powers and functions among federal, state and local governments. This wistful notion—known in political science circles as the "layer-cake absolute"—has never existed in reality but can be tracked back to some of the pro-Constitution positions that James Madison expressed in the *Federalist Papers*. Said Madison: "The federal Constitution forms a happy combination . . . the great and aggregate interests being referred to the national, and the local and particular to the state governments." That created the freedom to quarrel about which interests were great, which aggregate, which particular, which local. Americans have been arguing about them ever since, but the "happy combination" has never taken place.

The federal system was messy from the beginning. Literate Americans were sharply aware of the confusion of powers the Constitution would create. States'-righters like Patrick Henry knew that a pre-eminent national Government was proposed. Said he: "This Government is not a Virginian, but an American Government." Nationalists like James Wilson clearly declared that the Constitution was to serve not theory but people: "Can we forget for whom we are forming a Government? Is it for men, or for the imaginary beings called states?" Indeed, arguments over the mess the Constitution was about to create grew so strenuous and disconcerting that George Washington later confessed he had been ready to support "any tolerable compromise that was competent to save us from impending ruin."

Most Presidents, regardless of philosophical sentiments, have wound up with similarly practical attitudes. Washington did not let his qualms about state sovereignty keep him from reaching into Pennsylvania to stamp out the Whisky Rebellion. Thomas Jefferson did not let his earnest convictions about limited power keep him from highhandedly concluding the Louisiana Purchase: only a fool would have let theory stand in the way of such a bargain. Modern Presidents almost ritualistically approach the White House with fine intentions of curtailing federal power, but a search of history turns up no examples whatever of success.

History itself debunks the myth that the U.S. scheme of government was supposed to evolve toward the fulfillment of some orderly blueprint that existed in the minds of the founders. They were smart, but hardly prophetic enough to foresee the ever fluctuating economic, social, racial and environmental difficulties that have given the governmental machinery its present tangled shape. The reality of those problems, and governments' response to them, debunks the idea that the federal establishment has grown constantly because of the influence of some special cabal of consecrated nationalists. Indeed, governmental growth has been administered by Republicans and Democrats, by conservatives and liberals—even by such a devoted states'-righter as Republican Dwight Eisenhower.

Ike did at least enter office as a states'-righter in 1953. The story of his subsequent practices may be useful to ponder during the coming season of debate. By 1957 Eisenhower was explaining why he had abandoned his stand against federal expansion: "In each instance state inaction or inadequate action . . . has forced emergency federal action." Hoping to strengthen the states, he enlisted the Governors' Conference in setting up the Joint Federal-State Action Committee to conduct precisely the kind of study U.S. Governors have now asked for again almost a quarter of a century later: a reappraisal of government with an eye to realigning powers. The commission's proposals were hardly fundamental. Example: the U.S. might "consider" abandoning aid to states for the building of sewage-treatment plants. Suddenly Eisenhower had to deal with Governor Orval Faubus of Arkansas, who had activated the National Guard to thwart the execution of a federal court order for the desegregation of Little Rock's Central High School. Ike, who had always refrained from speaking against state resistance to integration, did what he had to do: he federalized the National Guard. So much for personal sentiment; so much for states' rights.

No segment of the nation has ever managed to be entirely faithful to doctrine in the federal-state issue. Over the years, as Professors Alfred Kelly and Winfred Harbison write in *The American Constitution*, "every economic interest, every geographical section, and almost every state expounded a theory of states rights to justify its opposition to the prevailing policies of the federal government. Likewise, every interest, section and state supported some federal measures of a strongly nationalistic character."

In the 1980s, happily, the revived argument over federal vs. state powers is not provoked by any issue as dangerous as some of the past. The main provocation is simply—or complexly, perhaps—the workings of the 500 or so grant programs by which the Federal Government aids, stimulates, coerces and sometimes distresses the state and local governments. It may be that the movement for reform can lead to some useful improvements and adjustments in the workings of such programs. It is even conceivable that some rearrangement of functions among the governments may result. The reform movement, however, is headed for disappointment if it sets out to overhaul the whole system with the intention of dismantling federal powers to increase those of the states. "The hopes of those who would do this," says George Sternlieb, a specialist in public policy at Rutgers University, "are illusions." Mere adjustments in the system will remain difficult as long as Government must respond to the needs of a society always in flux, particularly when ostensibly local problems continually accumulate into national problems.

It has always proved impossible, as a practical matter, to achieve even crude symmetry in the distribution of governmental powers. Perfection is quite out of the question, even as an idea. In reality, it is hard to assemble a dozen people, citizens or theorists, who agree precisely on what American federalism has been or ought to become. The only indisputable thing about the notion is that it persists as part of the American creed—which is exactly why debates over it tend to grow so inflamed.

Indeed, because of the mythic role of the idea of federalism—the power of the mere notion to arouse strong sentiments—every American leader must embrace it in one way or another to serve the necessities of his times. Thus F.D.R. hatched the New Deal under the slogan of "cooperative federalism," and L.B.J. promoted the Great Society as a program of "creative federalism." Was federalism transmogrified in either case?

By now, every realist should see that federalism is a wonderfully loose garment that allows the American system to seem properly dressed no matter what hodgepodge of arrangements the governmental apparatus is pushed into. It may be true that the states sometimes seem, as Vermont's Governor Richard A. Snelling says, "just administrative agents for the Federal Government." That cannot be so awful. The Federal Government, for its part, is nothing but an administrative agent for the people. Most of those people are like George Washington most of the time, willing to settle for any arrangement that is competent to protect them from ruin and assure their right to a decent existence.

—*TIME*, February 9, 1981

THE PUBLIC LIFE OF SECRECY

1983

"We are all, in a sense, experts on secrecy. From earliest childhood we feel its mystery and attraction. We know both the power it confers and the burden it imposes. We learn how it can delight, give breathing space, and protect. But we come to understand its dangers too: how it is used to oppress and exclude; what can befall those who come too close to secrets they were not meant to share; and the price of betrayal."

Just so, and aptly enough, opens the book *Secrets: On the Ethics of Concealment and Revelation,* a new study by Harvard Lecturer Sissela Bok, an authority on ethics and author of the 1979 book *Lying.* Scheduled to be published in February, the book is scholarly, cool, painstaking and analytical. Even if it is not likely to crowd out works of romance, sex, adventure and physical fitness, its subject could hardly be more fitting, at a time when the human urge for secrecy sometimes seems on the verge of getting out of hand.

Not that Sissela Bok wants to rid the world of secrecy. Far from it. She argues that the practice itself is neutral, only good or bad according to the purposes it serves. Says she: "While all deception requires secrecy, all secrecy is not meant to deceive." It is benign, for instance, when it helps human intimacy or the casting of ballots in democracies.

Such hospitality toward secrecy is doubtless widely shared. To consider it evil in and of itself would be a considerable inconvenience to the human species. Everybody, after all, has things to hide; the mind, psychology teaches, even conceals information from itself. It is probably the very naturalness of concealment that tempts people to carry it to excess. There is, in any case, no end of secrecy.

No beginning is visible either. It is hidden in the remotest past. The tactic of camouflage that is instinctual among animals has been ornately elaborated in the human race. But no animal could mimic all the varieties of mankind's surreptitiousness. Hidden or encoded information is the very mainspring of drama, suspense, excitement and adventure. The screening of information has always been indispensable to both war and peace, to murder and romance, to spying and spirituality. Extreme privacy plays a prominent role in the most ancient myths. Irascible Zeus, who intended to withhold the knowledge of fire from humans, was outraged when he learned that Prometheus had gone public with it. Zeus was so put off that he assembled a plethora of troubles and sent them down to mortals in the custody of Pandora. Everybody knows the calamity that resulted from the insistence on disclosure of Pandora's cargo.

Secrecy hardly fascinates mankind any more today than in the past, but it is certainly practiced more methodically.

The most thoroughgoing control of information is to be found in totalitarian societies such as the Soviet Union and China, where even weather reports can be highly classified by the government. But there is scarcely any shortage of dodging and hiding in the rest of the world. In the U.S., the concealment of information is carried out so routinely in so many pockets of society that the practice is accepted as part of the perennial social weather, hardly worth special attention. Americans indifferently shrug off the extreme privacy practiced by commerce, industry and finance; by professions like the clergy, law and medicine; by societies like the Ku Klux Klan and the Shriners. But they tend to sit up and take notice when secrecy of some sort erupts into drama and controversy: say, when a Congressman goes to jail because of the FBI'S Abscam investigation, or when a group of well-dressed

Japanese businessmen get arrested and charged with stealing computer lore from IBM. Such episodes remind the public of how the clandestine pervades society. Day in and out, most people accept professional prudence—say, that of the fashion or auto industries—as just part of the passing lifescape. People enjoying Coca-Cola, Kentucky Fried Chicken or Thomas' English Muffins give little mind to the fact that such products rely on legendary secret recipes that have been hoarded, perhaps, more closely than the H-bomb formula (which a number of amateurs have long since put together entirely from public sources).

Americans for the most part bridle at the concealment of information only when they catch government practicing too much of it. This response is easy to understand. Americans, after all, are early and often drilled in the creed that hidden government is anathema to democracy, and never mind that the U.S. Constitution was drafted in closed session. "Concealment is a species of misinformation," said George Washington, and U.S. political leaders ever since have publicly followed his cue. What they do out of the public gaze, however, is often quite different. That is hinted at by the fact that the classified federal documents in the National Archives run into hundreds of millions of pages. More than hints are available in histories of such disasters as the U.S. involvement in the Bay of Pigs invasion (after which President John F. Kennedy complained to one editor that if the press had only exposed the invasion in advance, "you would have saved us from a colossal mistake"). Democratic government's capacity for byzantine deviousness is probably best told by that epochal best-teller, the Pentagon papers—that "hemorrhage" of classified matter, as Henry Kissinger ruefully called it—which dramatized, in 47 volumes, just how far a government could go in clandestine and illicit duplicity.

The U.S. public tends to be generously tolerant of the withholding of material when it concerns military affairs.

Such tolerance gives Pentagon bosses a lease to play games that are not always strictly tied to military security. In one glaring example, the Pentagon went into a culprit-hunting mode a few months ago when somebody made public certain classified information: a budget figure, as it turned out, and a blue-sky one at that, interesting (and embarrassing) not because it endangered the nation's security but because it suggested that coming deficits would be much bigger than the Administration had yet admitted. More usual in the military's perennial game of hide-and-leak is the sudden declassification of scary intelligence about the Soviet Union at just those moments when the Pentagon is leaning on Congress for fatter appropriations. Nobody questions the need for military secrecy, but even military leaders realize that the hiding of information can be carried too far: postmortems on the failed mission to rescue the American hostages in Iran showed the rescue team to have been handicapped because of security so tight that one team element did not always know what the other was doing.

The practice of concealment can become excessive in any walk of life, but it is especially susceptible to being overdone when it is used purely to serve power, as in government. Officials, administrators, bureaucrats and legislators can come to enjoy the capacity to hide not only legitimate sensitive material but incompetence, wrong judgments and ethical transgressions. It is no wonder that in democracies as well as in tyrannies, government tends to expand its capacity to hoard information. The U.S., to be sure, took steps to check and curtail this federal capacity in the wake of the excesses surrounding the Viet Nam War, the Watergate scandals and some mischief credited to the CIA and FBI in recent decades. The Government has nonetheless already accumulated a good deal of momentum toward a yet greater capacity for keeping the public in the dark: in an executive order last spring, the Reagan Administration made the hiding of records easier for civil and military bureaus while, at the same time, undermining the 1966 Freedom of Information Act that was designed to give citizens better access not to secret but to "ordinary" Government information. Viewing particularly the Administration's move to restrict the flow of scientific information, Congressman George Brown Jr. of the House Science and Technology Committee says that the effect could be "to shoot ourselves in the foot."

One may be tempted to shrug off Government ways, consoling oneself with the cynical belief that even the most guarded information eventually leaks out. The trouble is that leakage is neither dependable nor always timely. "Three may keep a secret if two of them are dead," Benjamin Franklin said, and there may be truth to that. But such folklore is no substitute for a sensible public policy. The public *vs.* Government skirmish over how much classification there should be will probably go on forever and, in any democracy, should.

Secrecy is destined to persist as part of mankind's world in all of its political forms. Even though most often associated with deceit, acts of concealment can be both benign and indispensable to the protection of personal and public values. Secrecy may not be privacy by definition, but it is certainly essential to it. In totalitarian states, where Big Brother's eye is everywhere, privacy can be had only by the most meticulous practice of evasion and concealment. But throughout human history, people have relied on silence to safeguard the sacred as well as the intimate and personal.

Ultimately, the very nature of things is densely veiled. If religion arose to celebrate ineffable mysteries, science sprang into life to solve them. So it is science that has shown the universe to be an almost onion-like construct of secrets, with ever more of them lying under the layers peeled away. Atomic theory explained everything—until it was found that every atom contained entire worlds of other inscrutable particles that even changed their nature upon being observed.

Today the quark is hotly pursued. When caught and analyzed, will it turn out to be the ultimate answer to the ultimate secrets of matter? Not unless the dossier tells when the quark happened to come into being and out of what materials and by what power.

To imagine any general reduction in human secrecy is intriguing but oddly difficult. It is not possible to envision a world from which *all* secrecy has gone. Some people have tried. Philosopher Jean-Paul Sartre felt that "transparency" should eventually prevail in human affairs and claimed to be able to imagine a time when people would "keep secrets from no one." Still, anybody contemplating humanity as it is must wonder whether, in a thoroughly transparent world, the species would not suffer spiritual anemia and perhaps terminal boredom. It may be diverting to speculate about the future of secrecy, but it can only be frustrating in the end. The future is the biggest secret of all.

—*TIME,* January 17, 1983

WHY DOESN'T MY GOVERNMENT STOP LYING TO ME?

1973

The question so far as I know has never been given the kind of calm answer that might be of use in this day of government of lies, by lies and for lies. Because of this lack, I venture these few thoughts. Where can one turn for the answer except to reality?

Plainly it would be silly to submit the question to the government down there in Watergate, D.C. Some politician would pop up, not to answer, but to discredit the inquiry. Likely he would claim it was the Old Wife Beating Question thinly disguised. He would be wrong, however.

It is the OWBQ undisguised. But before we suppress it, let us pause: true, reasonable men squelch the OWBQ under certain circumstances. It invites self-incrimination, so is banned from the prosecutor's arsenal. Fair enough. But we cannot fail to see that it is always the counsel for the husband who objects, seldom a freshly battered wife. So isn't it possible that the OWBQ is legitimate when asked by the victim spouse? Her motives are nicer than the lawyer's. She does not need to vindicate an unconscionable fee. No professional vanity sends her swinging on the cobweb trapeze of jurisprudence. Above all she doesn't need to trick her husband into incriminating himself: his excitable disposition is amply proved by her split lip. Nor is she necessarily vindictive. Wives historically hunger less for vengeance than for groceries, and in the end usually join in the husband's defense.

From the wife, then, the OWBQ is fair. Without apology and out of pure primordial wonder she can ask: Why doesn't that son of a bitch stop beating me? Who would deprive her of whatever relief might come with an answer? Who would even suggest she is not entitled to ask?

In a kindred spirit I ask why our government doesn't stop lying to us. I suggest an answer only for a kind of primitive relief. Broadly the reason is: *our government doesn't stop lying to us because if it stopped, everything would fly apart.*

Even brief reflection shows this to be self-evident. Assume the government inadvertently told Americans this truth: your desires do not have a goddam thing to do with what the government does. The result—riotous protest—would be predictable. The government must avoid this truth. The result—lies—is predictable.

This answer is self-evident but incomplete. Even the question is incomplete. The nature of the subject places it under the Axiom of Pairs, derived millennia ago on the ancient (and, alas, now vanished) Island of Tututango. Also called the Axiom of Tututango, it has come down to us in slightly distorted form: It takes two to tango. The axiom applies to any number of uniquely human activities: bribery, robbery, murder, adultery, wife beating.

It also applies to lying. "Lie" is an intransitive verb but an inherently transitive act. Our question therefore is not complete until we also ask: Why do we go on letting our government refuse to stop lying to us? Broadly the reason is: *we go on letting our government refuse to stop lying to us because, if it stopped, the everything that would fly apart would include us.*

This may surprise and unsettle many citizens. Many will resist it, because it implies popular complicity in the government's lying. Such is the reality. Our rulers must lie because of the need of Americans to believe that they are self-governing. As an alternative, a wistful observer might suggest that the government actually carry out the desires of the people. This notion, at this moment in history, is pure fancy unworthy of serious analysis.

Popular complicity is not only the reality but is destined, barring some miracle, to go on and on. It is because of our complicity, of course, that some of us may flinch at the simple realities sketched here. Our resistance to the larger picture arises out of the same need that gives rise to the situation. It is a circular operation, hard to see from within.

The reality begins to emerge as we ask why we are so reluctant to call our lying politicians liars. We shy from this even when their lies are obvious. To detect their lies it is not necessary to be arrogant; one need not pretend to possess all the world's truth. The people of Tututango used to say: "I do not need to own an orchard to avoid eating a road apple." The truism needs no translation. Yet our politicians constantly feed us road apples and we keep calling them overripe winesaps.

Journalists take the lead in this dodging and veiling. *Rhetoric* they call the flatulent lies of the campaign trail. Thus they debase an honorable word to spare the politicians. The amiable acceptance of lying by rhetoric is taken as a mark of sophistication. Yet other, perhaps graver, forms of lying find our journalists reaching for other tender euphemisms. One commentator wrote a whole column about the Nixon administration's lies without once using the word. He spoke of "deception" and "evasion" and "double-talk" and "revealing half-truths." One half-revealing truth emerges when we ask why he could not simply say, "They're lying."

What is half-revealed by the question is fully bared by the answer. The journalist's reluctance is not a defect of personal character. It arises from the character of American journalism. It fulfills a tribal function. It burnishes, preserves and protects those verities and shibboleths that Americans cherish—those beliefs whose sum is the American identity. Journals that either dissect or coldly examine these verities and shibboleths are soon either defunct or doomed to marginal existence. Such are the "little" magazines that reek of alien ideas. They are not little by choice but because they are unorthodox and so get no support either from large numbers of citizens or prosperous corporations.

So, inevitably, the commentator reaching for a mass audience plays to a constituency that coincides with the government's. Handing out raw truth that tends to undermine the verities costs him his following first and his job second. Hence the "temperate" voice is revered in editorial offices and studios. One whose language grows blunt is derided as "shrill" and is eventually ostracized. Clearly the standard of temperateness does not rest merely upon civility and humility. Savagery is still admired when the critic is merely tearing apart the product of individual creation, a play or a novel. The "temperate" voice is mandated, however, when the subject is the nation and government. The mandate is an outgrowth of prudence: no readers, no ads.

Therefore, back when Lyndon Johnson was spinning an epic web of lies, the best American journalists could do was to begin speaking of a *widening* Credibility Gap. Ha, ha. But of course this did not describe the phenomenon that was actually taking place: a temporary *decrease* in the journalists' Gullibility Index. Journalism was trapped in its previous temperate depiction of Johnson. He actually remained quite as credible as he had been from the start. But I recall only one writer, Robert Sherrill, author of *The Accidental President*, showing nerve enough to go into print calling LBJ what every journalist deserving of the name knew him to be: a liar.

The popular journalism's (not conscious, but organic) function is more to divert us from than to disclose basic, unsettling truths. The tube ever flickers with factual truths whose sum is naught. Like the papers, it gives us dazzling lights bounced off a prism, gleaming and enchanting but, however turned, opaque. The very character of the "news" diverts us from larger realities. Thus, news of corruption blinds us to the reality that the submerged matrix of the news is itself corrupt. Only the *surfacing* of corruption excites the journalist. And he gives us the impression that some corrupt fragment is novel—an exceptional *blip* along an even seismic line of constant rectitude.

Blip came the ephemeral tales of Dita Beard and her memorandum, of the ITT and its document shredders, of the White House and its aggressive hospitality to the company's insatiable yearning for growth, of the pliant Justice Department. A cartoonist could tell the whole story by showing ITT lumbering about with the White House and the Justice Department in its billowing pocket. But what was really revealed?

Not much that was new. A U.S. Senate committee heard the story with fastidious patience and impregnable indifference: it was not surprising, merely diverting. If, as alleged, ITT had been mindful of its need for a favorable ruling from the Justice Department on its expansion plans, if indeed it had thought primarily of this when it pledged $200,000 to finance Nixon's next convention—so what? In a society that takes its fee-prone ethic from the purchasing agent and the broker, what prevalent principle was violated?

So the ITT case was, in reality, a story without suspense. The only mystery was why ITT felt disposed to pay the Republican party for the public interest when the party exists to give it away. The important lesson of the story was about a corruption of identity: beneath their formal surfaces, wherein they appear distinct, the government and ITT (among other vast organizations) function as one. Here was the source of the temporary discomfiture of the American people: our essential illusion of self-governance was breached. Then swiftly it was repaired.

How? When it seemed that the people—against their wish—might learn that the government is inseparably in bed with ITT, journalism came to the rescue. It portrayed ITT and government as adversaries circling and maneuvering. Presto: soon the distinct identities dissolved by the facts were restored by the drama. So it goes.

Americans cannot bear a regular diet of reality. Suppose the President spoke as plainly as did Robert Townsend, the former corporation executive who has taken to "blowing the whistle" as a public service. He draws a picture of things that can be verified by anybody with unsentimental eyes. Townsend writes that:

> America is run largely by and for about 5,000 people who are actively supported by 50,000 beavers eager to take their places. I arrive at the round figure this way: maybe 2,500 megacorporation executives, 500 politicians, lobbyists and Congressional committee chairmen, 500 investment bankers, 500 commercial bankers, 500 partners in major accounting firms, 500 labor brokers. If you don't like my figures, make up your own, we won't be far apart in the context of a country with 210 million people. The 5,000 appoint their own successors and are responsible to nobody. They treat this nation as an exclusive whorehouse designed for their comfort and kicks. The President of these United States, in their private view, is head towel boy.

It is not easy to imagine the President going that far. He would likely feel that the part about "towel boy" demeaned, not the occupant, but the office. But of course no minion of government would come within a million miles of this crude but essentially truthful picture of things. Why? Such a truth coming from a tribal leader would make Americans restive, to say the least.

Not that Americans are incapable of glimpsing the truth. Our very folklore reflects our awareness of the accuracy of Townsend's picture of things. "It's not what you know but who you know," we say, and "They never get the big boys."

Early on, most of us learn that greed and avarice are the driving engines of our society. We celebrate the rich man who has gouged the most out of his fellows. We are all aware that as a people we are obsessed with growing as rich as possible, with accumulating far more than we need. But what we like to *believe* is something else. We prefer the President to sing to us over and again of the nobility and humanity of the "free economic system."

Such is the devious intricacy of our need. We simultaneously know certain actualities while suffering this quenchless hunger for deception. Every schoolboy learns that his forebears got the nation's land and resources by trespassing, murder, massacre and pillage. And all but the witless must learn sooner or later that this country's strain of violence makes other civilized nations seem tame. Even so, imagine a political leader telling an audience of typical Americans this truth: much of the time we act like barbarians and beasts. What would the audience do? It would scream NO—and tear the speaker "limb from limb," to recall Martha Mitchell's prescription for dealing with the girl who spoke her mind at the White House.

It is the topical lie that we most notice, simply because we obsessively feed on the "news." It is these lies we prefer to call "dissembling" or "deception" or "evasion," ever avoiding shrillness. Thus we all enjoyed a public discourse over whether Henry Kissinger was lying when he said "Peace is at hand." This discourse was going on even as bombs rained on Hanoi in an act of unspeakable savagery. Solemn commentators were asking *whether* the administration might have deceived the people. Everyone seemed utterly incapable of seeing the lie that the merest child could spot. The public discourse was preposterous.

Why would our pundits protect the beasts in the White House? Or was that their purpose? Any reasonable man would assume that they could not have failed to see a bald-faced lie. Consider: they toiled, not to protect the lying rulers, but to save us from an unbearable truth about ourselves.

Unless we could suppose that Kissinger and Nixon *might* have been telling the truth, we would have no choice but to accept that we had all become something we could not bear to be—a nation of barbaric murderers. For we remain trapped—against all the evidence—by our ineradicable belief that we still rule ourselves. By the light of that belief, Nixon was not our master, he was our servant, as foretold by our verities and shibboleths. So he was *us*, and it was *our* hand pulverizing the life and landscape of a tiny nation far away. We didn't dare call him a liar.

It is out of the wellspring of fundamental lies that all of the topical lies inevitably flow. But our self-deception is scarcely unusual. Men everywhere at times choose a dream over unacceptable reality. The American Dream is what we call our web of fragile beliefs. But was it stuff from the American Dream or some different reality that fell out of the sky over Hanoi? Is it the stuff of the American Dream that we see in the hideous cities of the land? And what of our national decision to perpetuate millions of our fellows in unemployment? Is this reality extracted from the American Dream? Is our decision to leave millions in hunger? Our ever more vicious subordination of justice to order?

Why do we suppose that the President and his henchmen are at war with the press? Why do we suppose our rulers are emasculating the First Amendment? Is it because they merely hate journalists? Or are they really protecting the American Dream? Could it be that they fear too much of reality might somehow spill into the eyes of the people—and suddenly the old dream might die not with a whimper but a bang?

And so back to the main question: our government keeps lying to us as a favor to our averted vision. And our averted vision is a defense against unbearable reality. Thus we thrive as a blind tribe led by Lilliputians who mistake power for greatness and mechanical aptitude for holiness.

Ours will be known as the epoch when the explicable flight of a rocket became, in the eyes of Lilliput's emperor, the mightiest act since the unfathomable creation of the cosmos. In our day the dark eye of a mole is compared with a billion exploding suns.

In the ineffable reaches of space, our earth and moon revolve infinitesimally trivial, but we have lost all perspective. Billy Graham leads the White House in prayer to a God who applauds napalm, and Washington leads us in worship of a corporate self whose body we do not perceive. Thus we publish the martial intents of God and take impenetrable mystery unto ourselves.

The miracle to pray for is this: that our very capacity to see or smell or taste the truth does not go the way of the Island of Tututango (alas, now vanished).

—*INTELLECTUAL DIGEST,* July, 1973

THE BUSTING OF AMERICAN TRUST

1980

"Trust is a social good to be protected just as much as the air we breathe or the water we drink." So argues Sissela Bok, a lecturer on medical ethics at Harvard Medical School, in her book *Lying*. Most Americans would readily agree. Yet Americans are finding it ever more risky to trust the world about them. Duplicity crops up so often and so widely that there are moments when it seems that old-fashioned honesty is going out of style.

That is certainly not the case. Most Americans are dependable and forthright—most of the time. Enough people fall short of square dealing, however, to have left Americans a keen hunger for someone to trust. While political lying may have entered an "era of mass production," as Critic Robert Adams says in *Bad Mouth*, the problem of deception goes far beyond politics. Many people in academia, in science, in engineering, in medicine, in law, in the crafts—all have been caught in the act of exercising the scruples of a fly-by-night lightning-rod salesman. Skulduggery turns up so often in the commercial world that the best graduate schools of business train students to cope with deceptive practices. Americans as a whole so stretch the truth in preparing their tax returns that the Internal Revenue Service claims that it cost the U.S. Treasury at least $18 billion last year. An obscure copy editor at the New York *Herald Tribune* coined the phrase Credibility Gap 15 years ago to jazz up a headline over a story about L.B.J.'s Washington. Today Credibility Gap appears to span the continent.

Honesty, as Diogenes would caution, has never been the strong suit of the human species. Mandatory oath taking in legal proceedings was not invented out of faith in the natural probity of witnesses. Everybody fibs, alas. It is also true that every epoch has its roster of villains, its quota of predatory deceit. Yet today the roster seems far longer than usual, and most observers agree that the quota of duplicity—from artful dodging to elaborate fraud—is growing intolerably large.

Why? In addition to the ever present greed and the lust for special advantage, there are a number of reasons for increased deception. The general relaxation of moral codes is doubtless one. Another is the steadily growing pressure for personal achievement in an increasingly competitive world. The incentive to cheat is heightened by the fact that society is more and more an aggregate of strangers dealing impersonally with each other. Finally, there is the snowballing impression that everybody must be cheating.

That accumulating impression, though false, is what takes such a toll of social faith. The abuse of trust has become so commonplace that one must wonder whether society's very capacity to believe is not being gradually undermined. It has taken a drubbing in recent decades. Watergate yesterday, Abscam today. In between, the people's credulity has been hounded by far more than the usual con games and rackets. The pathetic fact is that Americans seem to be resorting more and more to preying, with methodical duplicity, on other Americans.

Only the young could be unaware of a change in the tone of many ordinary business dealings in the country. Twenty years ago the householder who called a repairman tended to assume, more often than not, that the job would be fairly estimated and honestly carried out. Today Americans are far more likely to feel uneasy when they find it necessary to deal with crafts of all sorts—home improvement companies, television repairmen, appliance mechanics.

Investigations of automobile repair shops have turned up such widespread hanky-panky that some car owners half expect to be ripped off when their vehicle needs fixing. Consumer complaint bureaus spend a good deal of their energy handling complaints about price gouging and false representation. The wish to avoid being victims, as well as the wish to save, has turned many Americans into do-it-yourselfers.

Duplicitous practices have also been staining the nation's most prestigious realms. Athletes at several Pacific-10 Conference universities turn out to have been the beneficiaries of a widespread traffic in bogus credits and forged transcripts, sometimes with the connivance of academic administrators. Surgeons have been caught prescribing needless operations and letting medical equipment salesmen suture incisions; one salesman even assisted in a hip joint replacement. Lawyers and doctors have turned up operating auto accident rackets to bilk insurance companies. Engineers have been found out faking X-ray inspections of joints in the Alaska oil pipeline. Enough—though there is much more.

Duplicity racks up innumerable specific victims, to be sure, but the more enduring results are not as easy to spot. The concentrated lying imposed on victims of brainwashing can eventually cause a mind, as Philosopher Hannah Arendt put it, to refuse "to believe in the truth of anything, no matter how well it may be established." Americans clearly have not reacted to widespread deceptions in that pathological way. Even if disenchanted, they have so far tended to become more mulish and skeptical as voters, more diligent as consumers and more strenuous as activists. They have, for example, persuaded Congress and state legislatures to pass a large collection of truth-in-almost-everything laws to ward off duplicity in such activities as lending, labeling and advertising.

Still, some ill effect has been achieved when a nation becomes obsessed with and doubtful about the credibility of just about everybody and everything. One thing that has become more constant than corruption, says Robert O'Brien, a Massachusetts Consumers Council executive, is "the expectation of corruption." Such deepening doubt can be seen as both cause and effect in the everyman-for-himself spirit that has tended to show itself since the early 1970s—at great cost to the spirit of community. Americans in the best of times must cope with a world designed to confuse the powers of belief and disbelief. Theirs is a huckstering, show-bizzy world jangling with hype, hullabaloo and hooey, bull, baloney and bamboozlement. The supersell of some advertising and the fantasies that stutter forth from TV are enough to keep credulousness off balance.

Today's sheer quantity of disinformation suggests that the people best equipped to cope with contemporary life might be the Dobu Islanders of Melanesia: they habitually practice deceit on everybody and exult in the craft of treachery. Anthropologist Ruth Benedict, who chronicled the ways of the Dobu tribe in *Patterns of Culture*, noted that, in their eyes, a "good" and "successful" man was one "who has cheated another of his place." The U.S. is far from living by any such absurd, upside-down ethic. Yet, in the light of today's trends, it can do no harm to ponder the price society pays for the incessant abuse of trust.

—*TIME*, October 20, 1980

FIVE

While America Slept:
The Turbulent Peace Between The Wars

Some Cases Never Die, Or Even Fade

W.W. II: Present And Much Accounted For

The Marshall Plan: A Memory, A Beacon

An Account Of Some Conversations On U.S. 45

The South

The Hesse Trip

The '70s: A Time Of Pause

Looking For Tomorrow (And Tomorrow)

WHILE AMERICA SLEPT: THE TURBULENT PEACE BETWEEN THE WARS

1989

America's everyday face in 1939 did not suggest a nation with war on its mind. Two festive world's fairs were going simultaneously, one in San Francisco, the other in New York City. People were lining up for nifty flicks like *The Wizard of Oz, Gone with the Wind, Goodbye, Mr. Chips,* and *Mr. Smith Goes to Washington.* Royalty-loving Americans got a double thrill when the King and Queen of England dropped over to visit President and Mrs. Franklin D. Roosevelt at their Hyde Park residence; the King had hot dogs and beer.

Diversion of a heavier sort was provided by World Champion Joe Louis: he handily trounced beer-guzzler Two-ton Tony Galento. There were other scraps: Mrs. Eleanor Roosevelt resigned from the Daughters of the American Revolution when it refused to let Marian Anderson, a black singer, perform in Constitution Hall. Radio's Major Bowes manned the gong on his popular Amateur Hour. Book stores were selling John Steinbeck's *The Grapes of Wrath* and Carl Sandburg's *Abraham Lincoln: The War Years.* Singer Kate Smith, who in 1938 had gotten Irving Berlin to write *God Bless America* exclusively for her, had just about turned it into an unofficial national anthem. Clarinetist Benny Goodman reigned as the King of Swing, and Thomas E. Dewey, New York's gang-busting prosecutor, was identified as Republican Glamour Boy No. 1.

True, it was crisp news when, after his Easter break, the President left Warm Springs, Georgia, with an ominous promise: "I'll be back in the fall—if we don't have a war." Still, that possibility did not head the list of social concerns. The number one problem was the fact that 17.2% of the work force—almost 10 million workers—was still jobless. Ten years after it began, the Great Depression was far from over. A third of the nation remained, in FDR's clarion phrase, "ill-housed, ill-clad, ill-nourished."

Yet war did intrude on the popular mind. Most Americans were not surprised when it broke out in Europe. At least 51% expected war in 1939. Even more, 58%, were convinced that if war came the U.S. would be drawn into it. Those opinions were rounded up in January by George Gallup, an Iowa journalism professor who had developed public pulse-taking as a tool for advertisers. While politicians remained wary isolationists, 65% of Americans favored boycotting Germany. And 57% wanted the U.S. to supply war goods to England and France, which would take a revision of the 1935 Neutrality Act that Congress refused when Roosevelt requested it. Ordinary Americans were ahead of their leaders in sensing the realities of the world of 1939. Most did not dread war—as their passionate warmaking would later prove. Intuitively, Americans knew that war would give the nation a binding purpose it had long lacked.

Bracketed by world conflict, the period November 11, 1918 to September 3, 1939, can be viewed as postwar or prewar (or a bit of both) but not quite as peaceful. America may have slept, in a sense, while the clouds of World War II gathered, but the nation's life often seemed like a waking nightmare. The era was continuously turbulent, racked by natural disaster and man-made calamity, torn by bloody strife and hateful bigotry. Bitterly disillusioned by the shabby results of the World War President Woodrow Wilson had inspired them to idealize, post-war Americans needed strong leadership. Under sporting Warren Harding, mean-spirited Calvin Coolidge and unimaginative Herbert Hoover (who was never heard to laugh out loud by one long-time friend), they got government that was indifferent, inept and frequently corrupt. "Not since the fateful decade of the 1850s," write Henry Steele Commager and Richard B. Morris, "had there been so egregious a failure of leadership in American politics."

Hard times were not the exclusive franchise of the Great Depression. Throughout the booming 1920s, most Americans merely subsisted or lived in poverty. The average industrial wage, $1,158 in 1919, rose to $1,304 in 1927; minimum need for family of four was about $2,000. In mid-decade, some 6 million families (out of a total 26 million) were "chronically destitute." The between-the-wars era, 1920s and 1930s, was also bedeviled by politicians who incessantly whipped up popular phobia about communism; often they were even more vicious than U.S. Sen. Joseph McCarthy when he poisoned the 1950s. In the merest hint of what was to come, the Mayor of New York, promptly after the Armistice, forbade the showing of the red flag and ordered police to break up "all unlawful assemblages"—which turned out to be any the cops did not like.

History filters into America's folk memory through a soft focus lens. Recalling the post war era Americans tend to think of the flappers and the Charleston, not the Spanish influenza epidemic that swept the U.S. as the war ended, killing 550,000 Americans—five times the number lost in the war. Nor of the fact that in 1919 there were some 3,000 strikes that left, in Historian Geoffrey Perrett's words, "a heritage of fury that was to torment organized labor throughout the Twenties." Nor of the fact that the Klu Klux Klan blossomed in the north and south, more or less owned Indiana and Oklahoma, and flogged and abused and sometimes killed thousands of victims with impunity. Klansmen liked to wear, in addition to sheets and pointy hats, little "100%

American" buttons—odd, since hate in America usually prefers a flag in its lapel. Through the between-the-wars era, popular culture was flagrantly racist, portraying blacks as shiftless, ignorant and laughable—*a la* Hollywood's dimwited Stepinfetchit and radio's mush-mouthed Amos and Andy. True, the era did go crazy over that knee-knocking dance, the Charleston (originated in a black revue called *Running Wild*). Also over jazz and shortened skirts and bobbed hair for women and an easy morality that arose partly out of the spreading Freudian gospel. But the era also brought Prohibition with all its grotesque fringe benefits—bootleggers, speakeasies, gangsterism, pervasive hypocrisy, universal corruption, contempt for law. Racket had always meant an easy-money job; now the term racketeering in its modern sense entered the U.S. vocabulary. Chicago, where Al Capone ran the mob and cops too, was afflicted, "with such an epidemic of killings as no civilized modern city had ever before seen." So Frederick Lewis Allen wrote, adding that the Windy City chalked up some 500 gang murders in one decade.

Meanwhile, the radio and the automobile boomed simultaneously, beginning a radical reshaping of the nations habits and folkways. Sinclair Lewis published *Main Street*. Louis Armstrong recorded *West End Blues*. Babe Ruth inspired a renaissance in baseball, which the Black Sox scandal had left flattened. Red Grange became the first athlete on *TIME's* cover. Al Jolson starred in the first all-talky movie, *The Jazz Singer*.

The 1920s decade has been variously labeled: the Roaring Twenties, the Jazz Age, the Prosperity Decade, the New Era, the Lost Generation, the Incredible Era, the Era of Wonderful Nonsense, the Ballyhoo Years, the Dry Decade. It is surprising nobody has ever named it for rampaging jingoism. The era produced it wholesale. When it surfaces, the nation's Americanoid jingo spirit lunges forth flapping flags, belching anthems and demanding oaths of loyalty all around. That spirit took over all too many federal and state officials including Wilson's Attorney General, A. Mitchell Palmer. During hostilities, Palmer had imprisoned thousands of Americans (including Socialist Presidential Candidate Eugene Debs) for opposing the war or suspected German sympathies. In 1920, exploiting a wartime Sedition Act so loose it made practically anything illegal, Palmer decided that Reds were about to take over the country. Launching what his critics called the "White Terror," Palmer ordered a roundup of "radicals," and in a single night, without warrants, his agents arrested more than 6,000 persons—with a total of three revolvers among them. "In Hartford, Connecticut," Historian Arthur Schlesinger Jr. recorded, "visitors at the jail inquiring after friends caught in the raid were themselves arrested on the ground that this solicitude was prima facie evidence of Bolshevik affiliation."

Red witch-hunting was pursued recklessly all over the U.S. The New York legislature arbitrarily expelled five legally elected Socialist members—to the applause of The New York *Times*. "It was an American vote altogether, a patriotic and conservative vote," declared the *Times*. "An immense majority of the American people will approve." Kansas handed a 10-year prison sentence to Mrs. Rose Pastor Stokes, a feminist and socialist, for saying: "I am for the people and the government is for the profiteers." And gave her another 10 years for advising women not to bear sons, because they only would become cannon fodder. Thirty-two states passed criminal syndicalism laws. Local vigilance committees screened schoolteachers for loyalty, and hundreds lost jobs for reading the wrong books, having the wrong friends, holding the wrong opinions.

Chicago sent a score to jail for "Bolshevism"—after an undercover man testified one had an American flag on his toilet floor. In Connecticut, Clothing Salesman Joseph Yenowsky merely tried to discourage a bond salesman by criticizing capitalism and John D. Rockefeller—and received a six-month sentence. In Hammond, Indiana, a jury took two minutes to acquit Frank Petroni of murder after he testified the man he killed had said, "To hell with the United States." In Washington, a stadium crowd broke into applause when a sailor fired three shots into the back of a man who had not risen for *The Star Spangled Banner.*

Arrests of "radicals" routinely ran about 200 per week. Illegal procedures were common place. Some 800 suspects arrested in Detroit were held incommunicado for 10 days. More than 400 persons seized in New England were marched in chains through the Boston streets before being confined. Police considered solid information as unnecessary as warrants. One tip that foreigners were meeting at night led to a raid on a bakery at Lynn, Massachusetts—and the apprehension of 39 bakers starting up a co-op business.

In 1922 Katharine Fullerton Gerould wrote in *Harper's;* "America is no longer a free country in the old sense; and liberty is, increasingly, a mere rhetorical figure. No thinking citizen, I venture to say, can express in freedom more than a part of his honest convictions." William Allen White, journalist and sage of Emporia, Kansas, loathed what was going on, writing: "What a sordid decade. It will be known in American history 50 years hence as the time of terrible reaction."

It may be nobody has named the 1920s for its xenophobia and jingoism simply because the lunacy persisted through the 1930s. In the fall of 1935, Political Analyst John T. Flynn wrote: "No one can move about America without being aware of the deep breathing and pompous chest expansion of the one-hundred percenters. Any public proposal that seems to hit some entrenched interest is promptly branded as 'un-American' or 'communist.' As soon as that label is tacked on a proposal or movement, further argument becomes unnecessary." How did this sorry situation strike Americans who had just tried to save the world for democracy? "It was characteristic of the Jazz Age," said F. Scott Fitzgerald, "that it had no interest in politics at all."

Aside from money, what interested Americans, at least those who had bread, were circuses. Any fad or sensation or scandal would do, and the times abounded with them. There was a Mah Jong craze, a miniature golf craze, a tree sitting craze (not to be confused with a later flagpole sitting craze) which found boys roosting in trees day and night. There was an Eskimo Pie craze that sent world cocoa prices up 50% in three months. A cross-word puzzle craze put the phrase "cross-word widow" briefly into the vernacular. There was a knock-knock joke craze, or maybe epidemic is the word. There was a sun tan craze. A house trailer boom resembled a craze. During a long candid camera craze camera imports increased five-fold from 1928 to 1936. A feverish Florida real estate craze grew into epic frenzy before fizzing after a ruinous hurricane that also killed 1,838.

Sensational trials turned journalists into lurid aerialists and courtrooms into three ring attractions. In Dayton, Tennessee, came the notorious monkey trial, in which a defendant accused of teaching evolution was all but overlooked as Clarence Darrow, for the defense, demolished Fundamentalist William Jennings Brant, counsel for the prosecution and the Bible. Bryant died just three days after Darrow's client was found guilty. There was the preposterously sensational trial of the wife of the Rev. Edward Hall, accused of killing him and Mrs. Eleanor Mills along a lover's lane near New Brunswick. The trial inspired gothic classics of tabloid reporting when pig farmer Jane Gibson—alias "the pig woman"—testified to what she saw one night after a weird, unscheduled, moonlight ride down the lane on her trusty mule. Then there was the trial of New York Suburbanite Ruth Snyder and her lover, Corset Salesman Judd Gray, for braining Albert Snyder with a sashweight. Fortunately, what threatened to be a lull between Hall/Mills and Snyder/Gray was filled with the trial in which Frances "Peaches" Browning sought separate maintenance from her hubby, New York Realtor Edward

W. Browning, because of his penchant for giving young girls all of the delight of 20th century Cinderellas. Quite grave yet still sensational was the long-lasting trial of Nicola Sacco and Bartollmeo Vanzetti, two admitted anarchists convicted (wrongly, many believed) of a Massachusetts murder and executed in 1927. The Sacco-Vanzetti case aroused intense passions all over the country and world. Yet even in the year of their execution, infinitely more of American's attention was awarded to one man—Charles Lindbergh. Upon his dramatic solo flight to Paris, America treated Lindbergh to an immense orgy of celebration and adulation. It seemed the nation was desperately starved for a hero, which it was. Lindy—innocent, honest, unassuming, forthright—was everything the era was not, and the country came close to worshipping him. Similarly Americans indulged an orgy of communal grief in 1932 when the hero's son was kidnapped and murdered. Respect for Lindy, however, did not deter the avid press later from turning the trial of Bruno Hauptmann (convicted and executed for the kidnapping) into a carnival. And, ah! There was King Edward VIII's abdication for Wallis Warfield Simpson, the American divorcee. Here, in Polemicist H. L. Mencken's whimsical judgement, was "the greatest news story since the Resurrection."

About midway between the wars came what seemed the most prosperous year in history: 1929. It was truly bountiful—to some. At the time, however, the top 24,000 U.S. families had as much combined income as some 11.5 million poor and lower-middle class families. And fully 71% of all U.S. families had incomes under $2,500—bare subsistence for most of them. Unemployment that year was reported as only 3.2%, but the government routinely minimized the statistic by not counting laid off workers who might be rehired. The middle class was increasingly living on credit, too. Before the war little but houses were bought on credit. By 1928 credit purchases accounted for 85% of furniture, 80% of phonographs, 75%

of washing machines, 70% of refrigerators and more than half of sewing machines, pianos and vacuum cleaners. The obsessive stock market speculation fed by greedy dreams of ever more riches—that was the game of the upper crust.

That game ended, of course, in the Great Crash, which must be the best known event of the era. It was not a single collapse, but a long pitching slide that began on September 3—10 years to the day before the outbreak of World War II—and continued through November 13. The Great Depression that followed, contrived by a complex constellation of influence, is also embedded in U.S. folklore, a mythic happening. Superb pictures taken by photographers sent around the country in one of the New Deal programs have shown younger Americans the mood of the Depression, its desolate landscape, its wracked posture, the travail creased into the faces of those who endured its heartbreak.

The Great Depression: Business leaders remain smugly optimistic. On March 7, 1930, President Herbert Hoover (whose old friends could not remember ever hearing him laugh out loud) says: "The worst effects of the crash on unemployment will have been passed during the next 60 days." Unemployment spreads steadily. In 1932 it reaches about 12 million—25% of the work force. Chicago's Special Committee on Garbage Dumps reports: "Around the truck which was unloading garbage and other refuse were about 35 men, women and children. As soon as the truck pulled away . . . all of them started digging with sticks, some with their hands, grabbing bits of food and vegetables." Thousands of desperate veterans march to Washington to demand early payment of bonuses. Hoover rejects them. With tanks and troops bearing rifles, bayonets and tear gas, General Douglas MacArthur drives the Bonus Marchers out of their ramshackle encampment at Anacostia, Maryland. The Washington *News* mourns: "What a pitiful spectacle is that of the great American Government, mightiest in the world, chasing unarmed men, women and children with Army tanks ... If the Army must be called out to make war on unarmed citizens, this is no longer America." Sweatshops at the time pay young girls 60 cents to $1.10 for a 55 hour week; J. P. Morgan avoids all income taxes in 1930-31-32; Treasury Secretary Ogden Mills grants abatements and refunds of $6 million to his father's estate, of which he was executor and beneficiary. Clifford Burke tells Studs Terkel how it was for blacks: "The Negro was born in depression. It only became official when it hit the white man."

The Great Depression: No other modern nation had such feeble provisions for the jobless, writes Schlesinger. Shacktowns called Hoovervilles proliferate. Thousands roam the country as hoboes. Western farmers form mobs to prevent evictions. Roosevelt swamps Hoover. Hope returns. Prohibition is repealed. Demagogues and dream-mongers win big followings: Louisiana's Huey Long peddles his "Share Our Wealth" notion; Father Charles Coughlin peddles anti-Semitism and his National Union for Social Justice; Dr. Francis Townsend, 66, of California, peddles a pension plan ($150 a month to all over 60 on condition they promptly spend it); he dreamed it up after seeing haggard women digging through garbage. Novelist-Radical Upton Sinclair, running as a Democrat for governor of California with a plan to end poverty, is defeated by a massive Republican effort that becomes the prototype of dirty campaigning used to this day. Federal programs like WPA help but fall short, proving work for around 30% of the jobless, leaving the rest to parsimonious charities of local and state governments.

The Great Depression: State legislatures do next to nothing for relief, but no less than 44 of them waste vast energy debating loyalty oaths and sedition laws. California enacts a sedition law under which around 500 persons are jailed. New York's senate passes a bill to put an American flag in every classroom. It passes 48-2 after Sen. Joe R. Hanley declares (Hey, George, dig this!): "We want people to respect the flag and if they will not respect it voluntarily, then we will make them respect it involuntarily." United Textile Workers strike up and down Eastern Seaboard; Georgia Gov. Gene Talmadge throws pickets into a concentration camp; the North Carolina governor puts National Guard troops at the disposal of the mill owners; Rhode Island also sends troops against the strikers. Reflects the textile industry journal, *Fiber and Fabric:* "A few hundred funerals will have a quieting effect."

The Great Depression: Roosevelt carries all but two states (Maine, Vermont) against Kansas Gov. Alf Landon. "If Landon had given one more speech," says Columnist Dorothy Thompson, "Roosevelt would have carried Canada, too." The depression goes on and on and on. Just when you think it might stop, it goes on and on and on some more.

The Great Depression: FDR's plan to pack the anti-New Deal Supreme Court is defeated. Even meager recovery is reversed in 1937 when business cuts production, killing 2 million jobs. In 1938, 10.3 million are jobless, 19% of the work force. Congress resists expanding relief. Roosevelt rejects the novel idea that the Federal government could spend the country back into prosperity. War breaks out. Washington begins huge defense spending.

("FDR and Congress," writes Historian Robert McElvaine in *The Great Depression,* "finally began to restore prosperity by spending on military needs at levels they had rejected for social needs." At the height of the war in 1943 unemployment, at 1.9%, would for the first time dip below what it had been in 1929.)

A goldfish swallowing fad starts at Harvard and spreads to campuses all over. Chinese checkers becomes the recreational craze du jour. People line up for nifty flicks like *The Roaring Twenties* and *It's a Wonderful World.*

—for *TIME* (unpublished), August 21, 1989

Some Cases Never Die, Or Even Fade

1979

Is any case ever closed? The question is irresistibly provoked by three moldering cases that blurted into the headlines in the past few weeks. Consider:

—Just 49 years after high-living Judge Joseph Force Crater was last seen stepping into a cab in Manhattan, somebody phoned New York City police that the missing man, declared legally dead in 1939, could be found having a drink at Pat's Emerald Pub in Queens. The breathless tip proved phony, of course, as do all 300 or so reports on Crater's whereabouts that the police receive each year.

—Almost 64 years after legendary Labor Agitator Joe Hill was executed for murder by a Utah firing squad, a retired union publicist named Leslie Orear has launched a campaign to persuade Governor Scott M. Matheson to pardon him.

—Fully 114 years after Maryland Physician Samuel Mudd drew a life sentence for complicity in the assassination of Abraham Lincoln, President Carter has exonerated him of guilt in his treatment of John Wilkes Booth's broken leg.

Cases of mysterious disappearances and controversial verdicts, of marvelous disasters and battlefield riddles, of private scandals and public tragedies—all can live on and on. They offer fields for debate long after the studies, investigations, decisions and acts that ostensibly closed them.

Obscure fact often mixes with popular fancy, fuzzing up the truth and perpetuating legend. The old story of Thomas Jefferson's rumored love affair with a slave is opened for fresh examination in a new novel, *Sally Hemings*, by Barbara Chase-Riboud. The late Agatha Christie's brief, unexplained disappearance during her first marriage inspired a fictional explanation in the book and movie *Agatha*, which intensified speculation about the case and could stretch it out for years to come.

Footnote-minded historians, to be sure, try to keep alive even the most obscure human misadventures. Yet certain cases thrive quite apart from the historical impulse that might keep them stirring in the public imagination. It is not mere fascination with history that has kept the British forever trying to solve the murders by Jack the Ripper in 1888, or Americans perennially intrigued with the fate of Amelia Earhart, the aviation heroine whose plane disappeared in the Pacific in 1937. Various speculations have made butcherous Jack out to be a perverted prince of British royalty or a deranged mid-wife, and have made tragic Amelia a spy executed by the Japanese on a Pacific island or still alive and living in New Jersey.

Apparently when a personality possesses certain compelling traits, when an event carries some content of morality or ideology or suspense or horror or romance, some ambiguity, even an engaging murkiness, he, she or it is claimed by the public and used as a source of everything from mythmaking to sheer entertainment. The phenomenon provides glimpses of the subtle human chemistries from which folklore is manufactured. To know how such mythmaking works is to be freed of all surprise when dramatic events evoke numberless theories to account for them or produce songs, plays and novels to celebrate, rehash and elaborate them.

Assassinations of high public figures almost automatically become cases that are never closed. There was no way that the Warren Commission report could have put to rest the John F. Kennedy murder case, or that the conviction of James Earl Ray could have concluded the case of Martin Luther King

Jr. As Jimmy Carter's action in the Mudd case shows, even the assassination of Lincoln was not a closed case as of 1979.

The files never seem to stay permanently shut on long gone heroes. Congress in the past few years has reopened the dossiers of Robert E. Lee and Jefferson Davis to restore U.S. citizenship to those two Confederate stalwarts. Military analysts and moralists alike still pick over the cases of swashbuckling blunderers. Was General George Custer a fit officer or a dumb egomaniac who assured his own annihilation by his foolhardy bravado at Little Big Horn?

Celebrated outlaws are also perpetual sources of popular revisionism. While the film *Butch Cassidy and the Sundance Kid* purported to document conclusively that the two bank-robbing adventurers died during a fling in Bolivia, some Wild West buffs insist to this day that Butch beat it back to the U.S. around 1910 and lived quietly with relatives out West. Jesse James stirred such a spirited blizzard of legend and myth that, after he was shot dead, subsequent generations were persuaded by transparent impostors that the St. Joe desperado was, yessir, still alive. Questions about James (Was he a Robin Hood or mere hood?) will long stay alive.

The sheer public craving for romance has kept alive the case of Anastasia, daughter of Czar Nicholas II, who may or may not have escaped the Bolshevik assassins in 1918; undying interest has given wide hearings to several claimants to the identity of Anastasia. The divergent ideological fevers of mid-century America guaranteed that the Alger Hiss perjury case would stay effectively open right along with the case of the executed spies Julius and Ethel Rosenberg. The arguments in both trials are still thundering forth in such books as *Perjury: The Hiss-Chambers Case* by Allen Weinstein (against Hiss) and *We Are Your Sons* by Robert and Michael Meeropol (for the Rosenbergs, who were indeed the Meeropols' parents). There is always the hope of posthumous vindication: Sacco and Vanzetti were executed in 1927, but only two years ago, Massachusetts Governor Michael Dukakis proclaimed that because of prejudice in their trial no stigma should attach to their memory.

Probably not even these cases will ever last as long as that of Joan of Arc. Five centuries after she was burned at the stake, every facet of her person, her trial and the surrounding events are still scrutinized and argued by lawyers, theologians, historians, mystics, psychologists, poets and playwrights. Even medical pathologists have joined in the continual replaying of the trial of the Maid of Orleans. In 1958 Scholar Isobel-Ann Butterfield and her physician husband John theorized that an advanced infection of bovine tuberculosis might have led to the phenomenon of Joan's hearing voices. Critic Albert Guerard was right when, in a review of one of the thousands of books about her, he said: "The last word on Joan of Arc will never be uttered."

True, most cases do get closed, passing into history and out of memory. That so many linger, alive and kicking, speaks mainly of the human urge not only to look at the past but to lug it into the present, reshaping it into folklore. Which is always handy to have around for nourishment and entertainment, in case the present goes dry.

—*TIME*, September 17, 1979

W.W. II: Present and Much Accounted For

1979

War, as Jonathan Swift put it, is that "mad game the world so loves to play." If the game is even madder these days because of the threat of nuclear annihilation, the world has learned to keep alive humanity's fascination with it by doing what both Homer and the Bible did so well: replaying the big wars at a safe distance. Almost 40 years after it began, just 34 years last week after it ended with the surrender of Japan, World War II, the biggest war in history, is thriving today with remarkable vigor in the minds and imaginations of Americans.

It is the subject of more and more solemn study and the focus of boundless popular curiosity. It has become a truly prodigal fountainhead of entertainment, inspiring everything from sappy comedy to high tragedy, engendering chillers, thrillers and even fantasies that have been coming forth in salvos of histories, novels, movies and television shows. Furthermore, say experts who keep an eye on such trends, although it has not yet given birth to a *Gone With the Wind*, World War II is at last supplanting the Civil War as the country's favorite conflict for probing, pondering and—to be honest—enjoying.

The U.S., to be sure, has always shown a lively interest in World War II, but in the past few years the American appetite for war lore has begun to seem downright voracious—and is being fed as though it might be insatiable. Bantam Books, for instance, has put out 31 nonfiction books about the war in the past 18 months, 15 of them at a single pop last March, and all as part of an ambitious plan to put both new and old accounts of the war on the racks continually and indefinitely. Reflecting the same market mood, subscriptions to TIME-LIFE Books' series of 20 World War II volumes have passed 780,000 and are still coming in. Meanwhile, a mere list of already available books on the war fills up a dozen type-crammed pages of *Books in Print*. In light of it all, it is no surprise that Herman Wouk's latest fiction, *War and Remembrance*, has occupied the bestseller list for 44 weeks, nor that this year's big novel, William Styron's *Sophie's Choice*, is haunted by echoes of the Holocaust.

But the world of print provides only part of the evidence of sharpening interest in the war. Novels such as *The Boys from Brazil*, *The Eagle Has Landed* and *Soldier of Orange* have found their way into the movies, and Ken Follett's *Eye of the Needle* is about to—even as he puts together yet another World War II saga. If World War II films have naturally been less numerous than books, they have also—ever since George C. Scott swaggered across the screen in *Patton* in 1970—tended to be more spectacular and ambitious. TV is cluttered with World War II documentaries and dramas, ranging from the recent six-hour reprise of Ike's war years to perennial showings of *The Commanders*. The popular real-life espionage book *A Man Called Intrepid* is only one that has been translated into a television series: Last September, 80 stations all over the country began regularly feeding out a 25-episode presentation of *World War II: G.I. Diary*, a journal of obscure heroism. Undoubtedly, however, TV's varied World War II material was highlighted by 1978's blockbusting 9 ½-hour series *Holocaust*. Now all networks, in the words of CBS Special Projects Director Mae Helms, are "trying to come up with their own *Holocaust*."

It is impossible not to wonder why the nation has got caught up in such a welter of war lore. True, some keen public curiosity needs no special explanation. After all, most Americans now over age 34 experienced the war in civvies if not in uniform: the war is their own story. There are, however, some other specific reasons for the new intensity of interest.

Partly, it is because an abundance of fresh information has become available lately through the disclosure of previously secret documents. Britain took the wraps off its secrets in 1972, and the U.S. did the same in stages completed in 1975. Authors promptly went lurching after never-told-before stories. A notable example came out last month with a most unwieldy title: *Ultra Goes to War: The First Account of World War II's Greatest Secret Based on Official Documents.* The secret: how the Allies did and did not use intercepted German coded information.

The U.S. shift away from confrontation with Russia to its present policy of detente has also impelled many scholars to take a fresh look at the cold war, that byproduct of World War II. Many of the origins of the cold war sprang from decisions made during hostilities. The Allied decision to halt Patton on his dash toward Berlin, for example, isolated the German capital and made it a focal point of confrontation in the postwar era. Says History Professor Robert Dallek of U.C.L.A.: "We have to go back. Where we are now is a direct result of what evolved during that time." To his own surprise, Dallek's newly published *F.D.R. and American Foreign Policy, 1932-45,* has sold, instead of a few volumes to scholars as might have been expected, 10,000 copies in three months. Says the author: "It's a hot topic."

It is hot for yet another reason, and that is the peculiar mood that has been hanging over the public for a while now. It is the fretful unease that is often attributed to bruises left by the Viet Nam War, the anxiety over the fragmented and amorphous texture of public esprit, over the conspicuous lack of any binding or driving national unity.

This atmosphere has made older Americans homesick for, and younger ones curious about an epoch of legendary solidarity and singular national purpose. The larger character of the time, its heroic texture, can be evoked by a simple iteration of the names of its outsized leaders and commanders: Roosevelt, Churchill, Stalin, De Gaulle, Marshall, Eisenhower, Montgomery, Bradley, Patton, MacArthur, Nimitz. It can also be summoned up by the war's slogans and crucial place names: unconditional surrender, D-day, Normandy, the Bulge, Anzio, Guadalcanal, Hiroshima, V-J day. Many a vicarious pilgrimage, to that lost time is being made these days, and among those who have noticed the fact is Robert Kane, a West Pointer who founded San Francisco's Presidio Press in 1974 to specialize in military books. Says Kane: "World War I no one cares about. World War II was the last patriotic war. We were attacked. We had a reason to get involved. It was a very, very clean war."

Many Americans, then, have simply found it refreshing, or nourishing, to look back to a time when, as Eric Sevareid puts it, "there were the white hats and the black hats." And surely now is the season for looking back, when most veterans of the war have entered those graying middle years when thoughtful retrospection becomes virtually compulsive. Now, as well, their offspring have matured enough to have some serious curiosity about the days of challenge and sacrifice and blood and glory that the elders keep bragging they went through.

All these amount to millions who, as it was put by Frank Cooling, historian at the U.S. Army Military History Institute at Carlisle Barracks, Pennsylvania, want to find out not only "what I did in the war" but also "what Daddy did in the war." Cooling is familiar with such quests. His institute has been so busy keeping up with groups studying World War II that it worries about falling behind on cataloguing war material it exists to preserve.

No mere handful of explanations can possibly account for all the motives of Americans who feast on World War II lore. Readers quite indifferent to the war might study a monster like Hitler, who could probably appeal to this psychologically conscious age even if he were only a work of fiction. And the countless students of the Holocaust must be drawn to it by an utterly inextricable mix of horror and disgust, wonder and mystification, at what mankind has done to mankind. It is not easy, or really possible, to sort out even the garden-variety sensibilities at play among the public consumers of all the cultural war goods. Surely those who keep shtiky *Hogan's Heroes* going as a TV rerun series differ from those who keep such volumes as Hitler's *Mein Kampf* and William Shirer's *The Rise and Fall of the Third Reich* moving off the paperback shelves.

A mere wish to be distracted and entertained would be enough to draw people to the vast multimedia tide of factual and fictional material. There is something there for every yen: battles on land and sea, adventures in the air and underground, home-front drama, tactics, strategy, diplomacy, ideology. In *The Fuhrer Seed*, a new political thriller by Gus Weill, there is even a dash of genetic fancy. Espionage is a staple, naturally, and even equipment is getting immortality: one new $45 book offers the definitive biography of the Sherman tank, specs included. Nor has there been any shortage, in all this, of what Military Analyst Drew Middleton once wryly called "the Fifi-Dupont-was-washing-her-drawers-when-the-American-tanks-arrived style of military history."

The flood of material must seem familiar in more ways than one to Americans who lived through the period between 1939 and 1945. The war invaded U.S. culture in books, plays, movies and songs long before the country got into the fighting. By 1945 Critic Burns Mantle complained of "a sort of war-play weariness" around Broadway, and moviegoers must have suffered a similar feeling. Immediately after Pearl

Harbor, Hollywood—so Richard Lingeman records in *Don't You Know There's a War On?*—rushed to register titles for prospective war movies. Not many of the era's flicks—*The Fighting Seabees, The Fleet's In, Wake Island*—are memorable except as museum pieces, but one endured as such a standard favorite that nobody tends to think of it any more as a World War II movie: *Casablanca.*

The war was well ended before material of the quality of *The Best Years of Our Lives* and *The Naked and the Dead* began to appear. A movie like *The Bridge Over the River Kwai*, reeking of war's futility, could not have been screened during the conflict, any more than the cynical existential slapstick of *Catch-22* could have been published. Detachment required distance in time, and even more time was needed for the development of the best war material that was to come, those meticulous historical narratives, say, in which the late Cornelius Ryan, beginning in 1959, captivated a huge American audience. Indeed in print and on film, Ryan's tale telling in *The Longest Day, The Final Battle* and *A Bridge Too Far* might be credited with warming the public up for the heightened interest that is maturing today. Ryan's stories became part of the accumulating national memory of the war.

The U.S. fascination with World War II is no more or less a riddle than mankind's with war generally. It is at once easy to understand and yet as perversely puzzling as human nature itself. On its bloody face, war might seem a thing any sensible person would wish to put out of mind. Yet people have always clung to war, remembering it, exalting it and habitually mining it for human truths. War, after all, cannot be surpassed as revealing drama: it intensifies, exposes and amplifies all emotion and yearning, bad and good.

Oscar Wilde professed to believe that war is fascinating because it is thought to be wicked. His theory: "When it is looked upon as vulgar, it will cease to be popular." Obviously, war's vulgarity has not yet vanquished its wickedness or the sense of adventure it engenders, even if vicariously. That aside, World War II is likely to remain a popular subject in the U.S. for a long time to come, if only because, for millions, it is still viewed as the nation's most splendid hour.

—*TIME*, August 27, 1979

The Marshall Plan: A Memory, A Beacon

1977

Britain's Foreign Secretary Ernest Bevin called it "the most unsordid act of history." To Willy Brandt, speaking later as Chancellor of West Germany, it was "one of the strokes of providence of this century, a century that has not so very often been illuminated by the light of reason." It was launched upon the world in Harvard Yard just 30 years ago this week—in what was surely one of the most momentous commencement day speeches ever made. Sunshine tattered through the decorous elms as Harvard staged its first normal graduation exercises since the end of World War II. The morning ceremonies that spotlighted the new graduates concluded with the awarding of honorary degrees. T.S. Eliot was among the recipients. Another was a white-haired man in a plain gray suit who rose in response to President James Bryant Conant's swift and eloquent citation: "An American to whom freedom owes an enduring debt of gratitude, a soldier and statesman whose ability and character brook only one comparison in the history of the nation."

As the assemblage surged to its feet in a warm ovation, Secretary of State George Catlett Marshall, who had commanded all of America's military forces during the war, bowed, accepted his doctor of laws degree and sat down again. In his pocket, ticking off the day like a hidden bomb, was a speech whose content would shape a new world era and dwarf by its magnitude all the fame that Marshall had so far won. That afternoon, when his turn came to make a "few remarks" during the traditional alumni ceremonies in front of Memorial Church, Marshall quietly took out his speech and read it to his audience. Thus was born the Marshall Plan, an epochal—and magnanimous—undertaking unmatched in all of history. Through it, in the space of four years, the U.S. would spend an unheard-of $13.6 billion to underwrite the economic—and in a sense, the social and political—recovery of war-torn Western Europe, defeated enemies included.

When Marshall rose to read his speech, the war had long since been won, but not the peace. By early 1947 Soviet adventurism had inspired the Truman Doctrine, with its pledge of military help to any free people threatened by Communist aggression. By April, after a long and fruitless foreign ministers' conference in Moscow, the U.S. Government abandoned all expectations of obtaining cooperation from the Russians—even in balming the wounds of war let alone in fashioning a new world order. In Asia, China was on the verge of falling to Mao. Of most concern to Americans, however, was Europe, which teetered on the brink of a general economic collapse that seemed beyond the capacity of her ever divided nations to forestall.

Marshall's words that day in June 1947 not only gave desperate Europe a reason to hope but also snatched the initiative in the cold war away from Russia. Marshall wrought a revolutionary departure in American foreign policy, wrenching the nation out of an isolationist disposition that tracked back to George Washington. The European recovery plan that bore Marshall's name—Harry Truman insisted it be so titled—set the stage for the primary defense arrangements in use today by the Atlantic community. Without the economic and political base created by the Marshall Plan, NATO could not have come into being. Nor, likely, would the capacity of European nations for cooperation today ever have blossomed. The ideas that Marshall set forth are, in fact, still making history. At least an echo of his spirit of innovation could be heard last week in President Carter's promise at Notre Dame to "create a wider framework of international cooperation suited to the new historical circumstances."

As far as Marshall's audience knew before he spoke, the Secretary of State would merely add his bit to the usual commencement pieties. No ballyhoo had preceded him; no Washington flacks had scurried about alerting the press that a "major" statement would be forthcoming. In fact, say some who were there, neither Marshall's typically spare language nor his earnest but dry delivery awakened that gathering fully to a realization that here history was being made.

"I need not tell you, gentlemen, that the world situation is very serious." the speech blandly began. "That must be apparent to all intelligent people." Then Marshall sketched Europe's devastation and economic disruption:

> *"The town and city industries are not producing adequate goods to exchange with the food-producing farmer . . . People in the cities are short of food and fuel . . . The division of labor upon which the exchange of products is based is in danger of breaking down."*

Europe, in short, was broke, shattered—and desperate. In April, Marshall had come back from Moscow convinced that the Russians had every intention of exploiting Europe's misery. Then in May, Will Clayton, his Under Secretary for Economic Affairs, reported a rapidly worsening situation. Immediately, Marshall had given George F. Kennan and his policy planning staff two weeks to draft a plan to save Europe. Under Secretary Dean Acheson, as well as Clayton, contributed heavily to the proposals that were boiled down into the 950-word speech. Now Marshall came to the meat of it:

> *"The truth of the matter is that Europe's requirements for the next three or four years . . . are so much greater than her present ability to pay that she must have substantial additional help or face*

economic, social and political deterioration of a very grave character . . . Aside from the demoralizing effect on the world at large and the possibilities of disturbances arising as a result of the desperation of the people concerned, the consequences to the economy of the United States should be apparent to all. It is logical that the United States should do whatever it is able to do to assist in the return of normal economic health in the world, without which there can he no political stability and no assured peace."

And then to the heart of it:

"Our policy is directed not against any country or doctrine but against hunger, poverty, desperation and chaos. Its purpose should be the revival of a working economy in the world so as to permit the emergence of political and social conditions in which free institutions can exist. Such assistance, I am convinced, must not be on a piecemeal basis . . . Any assistance that this government may render in the future should provide a cure rather than a mere palliative."

One final crucial point grew out of a wish to force European nations to cease their eternal bickering and begin working together toward a longer-range goal of integration:

"The initiative, I think, must come from Europe."

Afterward, Marshall wondered whether his message had really got across. Had Under Secretary Acheson been right in advising against using the commencement as a forum on the ground that speeches there were "a ritual to be endured without hearing"? The audience had received him warmly, at start and finish, but had broken in with applause only once—and not at the most significant place. Marshall, as he had confided to associates, had hoped that the speech would trigger an "explosive" effect.

In fact, it did so—not in the U.S., although it soon got behind the idea, but in Europe, where the response was instant. That same night, Britain's Foreign Secretary Bevin began arranging the conferences in which Europe's nations would assess their needs as a region and go to the U.S. with a program in hand. As Marshall intended, *all* of Europe—Russia included—was invited to take part. But Russia, after the first conference, refused—and declared war on the plan as another example of U.S. efforts to enslave Europe. Finally 16 nations joined in developing a program.

Meanwhile, in the U.S., the Democratic Administration and G.O.P.-run Congress began hammering out enabling legislation in a bipartisan mood fostered mainly by Republican Senator Arthur Vandenburg. Congress doubtless saw the plan in terms of cold war designs, and its passage was helped substantially by Stalin's hostility to it. President Harry Truman himself considered the Truman Doctrine and the Marshall Plan "two halves of the same walnut." He signed the law on April 3, 1948. Two weeks after that the freighter *John H. Quick* left Galveston Texas, with 9,000 long tons of wheat for France—the first item of a vast outpouring of aid that would eventually include machine tools, farm equipment and raw materials of almost every sort.

The Marshall Plan worked faster than anyone had thought possible. By 1951, Western Europe's industrial production had soared to 40% above prewar levels, and its farm output was bigger than ever. Western Europe's current status as a vigorous economic competitor of the U.S. testifies to the plan's effectiveness.

Today the Marshall Plan is only a bright memory. But the very act of recalling its historic impact raises the question: Would the U.S. ever again give itself to an undertaking of such boldness and magnitude? Surely some of the world's conspicuous difficulties—the food and energy shortages, to name but two glaring ones—seem deserving of comparable heroic efforts. Such problems so far, however, have inspired occasional grand rhetoric without matching action. So perhaps a better question is: *Could* the U.S. today even muster the combination of generosity, self-sacrifice and determined will that it dedicated to the rescue of Western Europe? Does the national character remain capable of that spirit?

Beyond doubt the American temper is strikingly different today from what it was then. After World War II, the nation enjoyed an almost cocky belief that it could do anything—and everything. Had not the U.S. just saved civilization? Did not the U.S. own the Bomb? Most Americans were eager to proclaim their nation the greatest. And they turned out to be perfectly willing to prove it—once they had been asked to. Americans of Marshall's day, of course, also had trust in their Government—and a certitude about their power to prevail that had not been crumpled by Viet Nam.

The loss of trust and certainty are major differences in post-Watergate America. The nation also, more than in the past, nurses cynical doubts about the Government's capacity to solve any social problems—those at home or abroad. Moreover, Americans of 1977 often seem confused, in the words of one scholar, "as to where and in what way American power and intelligence can be most usefully applied." The words are those of a man who happened to direct the Marshall Plan in Europe in 1950-51—Professor Milton Katz, now director of international legal studies at Harvard Law School. Katz nonetheless believes that granted the recovery of trust and some clear sense of national purpose, the country could still match the great deeds of the postwar era.

Most thoughtful Americans—particularly those old enough to have seen the nation at its best—are likely to agree. That adviser to many Presidents, Lawyer Clark Clifford, does. "I don't think there's been any radical change in the American character," he says. And ever buoyant Hubert Humphrey, mulling the Marshall Plan days last week, ventured a feeling that seems typical in Washington: "I think we would do it over again—if the same circumstances existed."

There, of course, is the crux of the matter. History never *quite* repeats itself. The Marshall Plan arose out of a specific juncture of event, public mood and leadership. And who could possibly guess when and how such an impelling convergence might occur again? Nobody. But it would nonetheless be hazardous to assume, if it did occur, that the American people would fail to yield their best once more.

—*TIME,* June 6, 1977

An Account Of Some Conversations On U.S. 45

1964

Mississippi had hardly a surprise to offer a native son returning after five years. The plane dumped down at Columbus, near the place where de Soto led the first white men into the land that has been white man's land ever since. A Hertz man wearing a sweat-drenched work shirt and a tight-lipped smile provided a black Ford with air-conditioned relief from the stuporous, clammy heat that overlay the countryside like a shroud of steam-washed lint. Within half a hour's drive northward there were the first intimations of tension and violence.

The second thing said to me by an old friend I saw after stepping out of the car in a shaded farmyard on U.S. 45 was this: "I sure hope your car doesn't have New York tags on it." The first thing she said was hello but the second was as natural as the first. "Ordinary conversation in Mississippi," one observer noted long ago, "smacks of manslaughter."

He had listened carefully. Mississippi's vocabulary of violence is varied and old. Almost before he learns to spell the words, a white Mississippi boy masters the braggadocio of racial conflict ("A nigger get smart with me I'll be on him like white on rice and turn that nigger every way but loose"), and he utters these words as clarion proof of his masculinity.

After covering no more than the 28 miles of blacktop highway, I was listening to Mississippians justify the assassination of John F. Kennedy ("He had no business going down to Dallas trying to stir up those people just to get votes"), and express an implicit hope for Robert F. Kennedy

("They proved it out in Dallas. They's always one that can get through. I tell you, little Bobby better not come down around here").

With as little effort—just listening—I heard threats of outright insurrection ("I mean there's gonna be some killing if these niggers start trying to get into cafes and things"), rumors that "every store in Starkville"—home to Mississippi State University, down the road a piece to the south—"has sold out every bullet they can lay their hands on." Only one thing I heard seemed the least bit unusual. A well-educated man of early middle years tensely put a challenging question to his wife: "Would *you* kill one?"

But much of this was as good-humored as it was natural. It flowed out amidst laughter and jokes and nostalgic reminiscence. The "nigger problem" has been the hobby of every good Mississippian for a century, and the current state of crisis only places ancient attitudes in a new context containing new and explosive potential.

The quality of fearfulness is what is new. Everywhere—in locales from Columbus to Aberdeen to Prairie to Meridian to Jackson—ordinary conversation not only confirms Mississippi's hostility to outsiders, but some Mississippians' fear *among* outsiders. Many residents are putting out-of-state license tags on their cars to drive to the New York World's Fair. In friendly seriousness three close contemporaries asked me: "Do they give *you* any trouble in New York? Do you let them *know* you're from Mississippi?"

Mississippians have always been as neurotically sensitive to criticism as they are nimbly resourceful at rejecting it all. "I guess you'll go on back North and write another bunch of lies about us?" a gaunt and sunburnt old acquaintance joshed. "I'm going to do worse than that," I said. "I'm going to tell the truth." I wouldn't, of course. But only because the truth about Mississippi lacks credibility.

Who would believe that one would repeatedly get a *qualified* answer to the question: would you condone murder? The question sprang naturally from the Philadelphia story: *assuming* that those three kids were murdered, would you condone it. "Well, we wouldn't condone it in one sense," began one professional man, "—we would feel *sorry* that they were dead, and if we caught them we might even indict the men who killed them, but we would also feel that they were asking for trouble when they came down here trying to change the customs of other people."

Never underestimate the Mississippian's capacity for elaborately approving something he is against or disapproving something he is for. Mississippi is officially a dry state; nevertheless, it has an official tax on the liquor whose existence is legally prohibited. This is only one blatant symptom of the state's moral and legal duality. This dualism lends a certain unreal quality of amorality and extralegality to life in the state; it begets those delicious paradoxes that drive the uninitiated to despair.

Who could lose his sense of humor with a man like the late Senator Theodore Gilmore Bilbo around—framing a florid tribute to the virtue of Southern womanhood in one moment and, the next, implying that she would cheerfully submit to every vagrant Negro should the white man fail to prohibit it by law. An absurdity, of course. Just like the Southern womanhood bit. There was certainly nothing in the early years of my generation to suggest the Mississippians, white or black, complied with the Seventh Commandment with much more fidelity than they lived up to the Fourteenth Amendment.

Mississippians do attend churches, of course; and far more regularly than they burn them. A Sunday in Aberdeen is as tomb-quiet as ever. More so. With air conditioning and closed doors, one can't hear the fundamentalist hymns flowing out to mingle with the heat waves on the sidewalks. Back in 1946 there was a guy at Ole Miss who could play

"Bringing in the Sheaves" to a conga beat, but I'm not sure he could afford that sort of irreverence anymore. Gossiping that Sunday on an oak- and magnolia-shaded street, I referred to "card-carrying Baptists," and the friend I was talking to said: "Shhhhhhhhhhhh. Man, you're back in the South now."

I intended no disrespect. Though I am not now a card-carrying Baptist, I have been. They put up their first church in Mississippi in 1791 and led all other fundamentalist denominations in providing the theological myths that prop up the racial mythology. In Jackson, I heard that the Citizens Councils these days were helping the schoolteachers of Mississippi explain God's policy to third- and fourth-graders by giving them this script to read:

"We do not believe that God wants us to live together, Negro people like to live by themselves. Negroes use their own bathrooms. They do not use white people's bathrooms. The Negro has his own part of town to live in. This is called our Southern Way of Life."

Mississippians love that phrase. Among sentimentalists it evokes an entire social mythology—vistas of white-columned mansions and Aunt Jemima scampering through the house waking everybody up with, "Mawnin', mawnin', mawnin'." David O. Selznick later lent Vivien Leigh to the myth. But it's hard to believe that today's gum-chewing Mississippi debutantes can accept the fantasy, despite their frothy gowns and the aura of genteel obsolescence that surrounds their dances in mansions around Natchez. After all, their daddies are automobile dealers and feed merchants, not so interested in the credentials of dubious aristocracy as in the black side of the ledger sheets. As often as not, yesterday's thin-lipped, self-conscious redneck is today's well-shod economic power in Mississippi.

Every white man takes an upbeat view of new industry. "We got around 300 employees," an affable foreman said enthusiastically of a new auto tailpipe assembly plant in Monroe County, "and they're all white. There's not a nigger in the plant."

Everywhere in Mississippi the economic overtones of white supremacy are as audible ("Now, my neighbor's maid," says a Sunday-school teacher, "gets $15 a week, but of course that's for seven days") as they are insistent. Delta plantation houses often look as though they were by M-G-M, but to many a delta Negro plumbing is still a distant dream. Niggertowns of sagging, paintless houses on unpaved streets starkly offset the neighborhoods of middle-class residences that house the ruling whites. Some of the white man's old paternalism survives, of course. "Hell, we treat our niggers good," says a wizened old farmer with a sly cackle. "We let 'em put new crocus sacks in their windows every year."

Gallows humor and all, this is the kind of attitude that has made Mississippi notorious around the country. Many Mississippians still accept the validity of Governor James K. Vardaman's image of the Negro as "a lazy, lying, lustful animal which no conceivable amount of training can transform into a tolerable citizen." Vardaman, governor in 1904-08, said that Negro education would "only spoil a good field hand and make an insolent cook," and white Mississippians, by and large, are still vociferously confident that time has proved him right.

That's almost the case today. There have been glacial changes toward equality elsewhere in the South. But not in Mississippi. It took an Army invasion to get James Meredith into Ole Miss and a military escort to keep him alive there for a year. What will desegregation of public schools take? "You can safely predict that Mississippi will be under martial law before the year is out," said one old friend at the close of a long evening chat. Many agree. There's not only the summer civil-rights campaign ahead. For the first time below

223

the college level, school desegregation is slated in three counties—Hinds, Harrison, and Leake—come fall.

Does white Mississippi accept this as inevitable? No. Will the state accept it as inevitable and do the logical thing? Logic? What is one to expect of a state that allots the task of picking its official song to a gaggle of real-estate men?

Nobody of influence—including the state press—speaks up to suggest that Mississippi simply accept a little change and get on with life. Only a few take the mild open-schools-at-all-costs position. Private hopes that Governor Paul Johnson might harbor moderate leanings have been repeatedly punctured. When columnist Drew Pearson accused Johnson of moderation last week the governor rushed out a statement coupling a denial with a tribute to the white-supremacist Citizens Councils.

What makes Mississippi so different? Why the total rejection of change accepted by sister states also governed by white majorities? What distinguishes Mississippi's white majority from others? Ole Miss history professor James W. Silver offers an answer in the title of a book he recently wrote—*Mississippi: The Closed Society.*

Fair enough. Silver delineates—with copious documentation—a society obsessed by orthodoxy, one that suppresses dissent where possible or, if that fails, tries to crush the dissenter. (Mississippi politicians would have kicked Silver out of Ole Miss years ago if he weren't protected by tenure.) This hostility to heterodoxy is matched only by a neurotic sensitivity to criticism that show itself in souvenir auto tags. They don't say: "Mississippi—The Magnolia State." They say: "Mississippi—The Most Lied About State in the Union."

Many lies *have* been told about Mississippi. Indeed, the entire white society rests—morally and politically—upon an elaborate mythology. The myth of the Negro's everlasting "biological inferiority" was only the starting point. Depriving the Negro of education as well as equality left him with no skills; the financial burden of a dual school system only meant that both would be poor; shutting the Negro out of decent jobs only makes him a veritable ward of the state—and, characteristically, white Mississippians condemn the Negro for the very welfare checks he is forced to rely upon as they damn him for drinking and fornication, among the few pleasures left him. Consumed by the fire of its racial passions, the white electorate takes little notice that its politicians, too often if not invariably, are inept at governmental science.

Methodically, resourcefully, and willfully, white Mississippi has subdued the black man. And now, at last, the black man dominates the white. Even in the subjugation that continues, the Mississippi Negro dominates the thoughts, the emotions, the politics, the conscience of the white man. By his presence he dominates the economy. By his plight he dominates the present. And by America's insistence on altering that plight he dominates the future.

"The question," William Faulkner wrote nine years ago, "is no longer of white against black. It is no longer whether or not white blood shall remain pure, it is whether or not white people remain free . . . We speak now against the day when our Southern people who will resist to the last these inevitable changes in social relations, will, when they have been forced to accept what they at one time might have accepted with dignity and goodwill, will say, 'Why didn't someone tell us this before?'"

Just as it once took the Federal government to free the slaves, and will take it again to free the Mississippi black from subjugation, so in all likelihood will it take the Federal government to free the Mississippi white man from his self-imprisonment. So be it. Mississippi was not without eyes to see it coming. As they themselves say of so many victims of violence: they are asking for it.

—*NEWSWEEK*, July 13, 1964

The South

1981

The American South is much changed in the last generation and is still changing fast. What it is turning into is clear enough. It is growing more and more like the rest of the country. As plain as the Holiday Inn motels and McDonald's restaurants on its face, the region is being Americanized, homogenized, technologized. Nowadays, as novelist Walker Percy says, "a subdivision or shopping center in the South is much the same as in White Plains." The nation has even begun to set aside the old habit of thinking of the South as a dramatically special place; Americans increasingly lump it in with that larger, indistinct southerly reach known as the Sun Belt. The long-familiar South, in a sense, is vanishing.

That is, part of the South is vanishing. Not the natural South—the terrain, the climate. Not the commercial South, which is bustling. Atlanta's airport rivals Chicago's O'Hare as the busiest in the United States; the Port of New Orleans recently displaced the Port of New York as number one in tonnage handled; Houston can fairly claim whatever honor attends convulsive business activity and badly governed urban growth. Nor is there any sign that, in spite of television's supposedly flattening influence, the drawls and twangs of the variegated southern accent will soon fade away. Widespread poverty, among other things, is far from vanishing from the South.

So what is being lost? The most striking thing the region has left behind is obvious: the South is no longer the bastion of legally forced racial segregation and white-supremacist social doctrine. But other fading features of the region are not always so clear. It is often easier to pin down what the South is becoming than what it is ceasing to be. Much of the South that is being overwhelmed by change can be glimpsed only by searching through a monumental accumulation of images—not all of them real.

The South has always incited those who depict the region to a good deal of fancy. While it is true that the entire United States has been given to fable-mongering, in the South the tendency grew into mythomania—a weakness for creativity so strong that it often infects even observers from the outside. The result is that when the South is run through a literary pen, it tends to emerge panting like Moonbeam McSwine or else Prissy screaming, "Lawsie Miss Scahlett, Ah doan' know nuthin' about birthin' no babies." The South as Dogpatch; the South by MGM, starring Clark Gable and Vivien Leigh; the South as a dance board for Shirley Temple and Bojangles; the zip-a-deedoo-dah cartoon South of Walt Disney; the South as *God's Little Acre*; the South as *A Streetcar Named Desire*—such are the phantasmal sources of much of the still current imagery of the region. Outsiders eat it up, and so do southerners. The city of New Orleans has turned the real streetcar named Desire into a shrine.

The profusion—and confusion—of southern imagery cannot be a surprise to anyone who pays the least bit of attention to the region. There has never been much demand for (and almost no production of) straightforward depictions of everyday southern actuality. The notion of the South purveyed by television shows like *Flamingo Road* is rubbish, but if imaginary miles could be measured, rubbish of that sort would be found to be not too much farther from reality than many much worthier representations of the region. Inspired while studying a few impoverished families in rural Alabama, James Agee produced *Let Us Now Praise Famous Men*, and although the book reeks of genius, it tells much more about Agee's hyperactive sensibilities than it does about the back-country South. Life in the rural South has never been so routinely exciting as to discourage an unusual number of its youths from volunteering for military duty—thus enhancing the South's reputation for patriotism. As a matter of banal fact, the southern boondocks tend to grow impassioned and lively only when transmogrified by the creative juices of writers like Agee or Erskine Caldwell, among others.

There are, as many a southerner has realized, many Souths. Not even the ones certified in history books can be taken without a grain of salt. The gracious and cultivated Old South was, as everybody should know by now, a fairy tale concocted by slavery's apologists before and after the Civil War. The New South that succeeded it was duly heralded toward the end of the nineteenth century, but it and the dozen or so other New Souths that came along later existed mainly in the imaginations of civic boosters and political blowhards. The contemporary South ought to be well understood, given the attention it got in the press during the years of desegregation and the civil rights revolution of the 1950s and 1960s; still, the very essence of news is that it excludes the ordinary. Finally, it is hard to develop a clear notion of the ordinary South without discarding a good deal of promiscuous imagery and widely accepted lore.

There is, as an example of dubious lore, the deeply rooted belief that southerners universally indulge in the telling of long, complicated stories. In fact, many and probably most southerners could not tell a long, complicated story if they tried; moreover, it is not hard to find southerners who are taciturn or even inarticulate. This small fact may surprise many Americans—including any who might also be unaware that the South is loaded with people who hate grits and would not touch possum with a 10-foot pole; who seldom read the Bible, let alone quote it; who would not get born again even if trading stamps were given away with the deal; and who are kin to people who squirm at the thought of families as sweet and suffocatingly close as the Waltons. Furthermore, and in spite of the region's entrenched reputation for wonderful hospitality, southerners are far more likely to offer a stranger courtesy, civility and a xenophobic glance than to invite one to supper for no good reason. Hospitality in the South, like hospitality in the North, East and West is for kin and friends—and strangers when there is cause to cultivate them.

It could be that some people have never mistaken the images of art and entertainment for the southern reality. Still, the penetrating power of myths should not be underrated, as is proved by the case of H.L. Mencken. That hardboiled iconoclast used to make sport of the skimpy cultural development of the South of his day while solemnly mourning the passing of what he imagined had been the far more cultivated antebellum civilization. Mencken had swallowed the Old South myth whole, as it turned out, and shown himself—as Jack Temple Kirby writes in *Media-Made Dixie: The South in the American Imagination*—"woefully ignorant of even the basics of southern history."

Ignorance, to be sure, is not always to blame for the spreading of certain forms of southern malarkey. Consider, as one example, the sweep of southern poet-novelist James Dickey's testimony of a few years back about personal deportment in the South: "Good manners and graciousness are a holdover from way on back, not just an aristocratic tradition but a southern tradition. I've been in dirt farmers' homes where they've been as gracious as a grand duke." (The rapacious, sodomizing hillbillies that Dickey depicted in his novel *Deliverance* were presumably exceptions to the rule of universal graciousness.) As another example, contemplate author Willie Morris's claims for the unique atmospherics of Mississippi in a recently published recollection of his childhood in that state: "We were touched implicitly, even without knowing it, with the schizophrenia of race and imbued in the deep way in which feeling becomes stronger than thought with the tacit acceptance that Mississippi was different, with a more profound inwardness and impetuosity and a darker past not just than that of New York, or Ohio, or California but of Arkansas, Tennessee, Alabama and Louisiana, which were next door." Oh, come on. While a child growing up in Mississippi would sooner or later realize that the state trailed the nation in everything except perhaps the hookworm rate, very few if any children would be likely to think *or* feel notions like "a darker past" until *after* reading William Faulkner. The point is that anybody who wants to glimpse the ordinary South ought to realize that the Mississippi actuality is to Yoknapatawpha County as the basic musical scales are to the symphonies of Beethoven.

Southern mythification has always taken many forms, and there are naturally many ways of accounting for it. Southerners, of course, share with all human beings the wish to make a case for their own specialness, the yen to make the common seem extraordinary. Beyond that, the South has long had special incentives for exaggeration and dissembling: for generations, white southerners could not bear to tell the simple truth about the subjugation and mistreatment of blacks. And then there are the incentives arising out of the South's lower standard of living, as Paul M. Gaston points out in *The New South Creed*. Says Gaston: "One of the reasons for the superabundance of southern myths is that southern life has involved such a high degree of failure and frustration that intellectual and emotional compensations have been at a premium."

What harm, if any, has resulted from southern mythmongering and yarn-spinning is impossible even to guess. One effect of the continual overdose of overblown imagery has been easy to sense, however. It is a certain weariness with distortion, a certain frustration, a certain wish to obtain some clear, sure notion of the simple, everyday South. After all, there is such a South, a place in which neither Sartorises nor Snopeses are numerous enough to be noticed: a world that exists with little melodramatic emphasis, its days filled with simple work, simple pleasures, simple devotions; a region peopled by inconspicuous individuals little given to brooding about the South's past (tragic, dark or otherwise) and certainly not given to brooding in Faulknerian sentences.

That South has always existed, being the everyday South of ordinary people. Because of the smaller scale of its peregrinations and the diminishing profit to be found in its exploitation, it is indeed being squeezed aside by modern high-rise civilization. That South may or may not be literally vanishing, but it has for a long time been hard to find.

—*GEO*, December, 1981

The Hesse Trip

1971

"The true profession of man is to find his way to himself," said Hermann Hesse. Since I agree with those 12 plain words, it was as a professional in more ways than one that I finally took the trip, the one so many Americans have taken lately, the Hesse trip, a sojourn to a mind ceaselessly self-searched by its tenant, all his long life.

Hermann Hesse was born in Germany in 1877. He died at 85 in Switzerland. By trade, he was a writer. T. S. Eliot, Andre Gide and Thomas Mann considered him a master. So, presumably, did the Nobel Prize committee. He won the Nobel in 1946. At his death, however, few Americans had read him. In fact—

"To American readers," said the New York *Times* in Hesse's obituary, "he remained largely unapproachable despite a flurry of interest in his novels after the award of the Nobel Prize.

"Perhaps it was because of the profound spiritual themes that preoccupied him most of his life or the melancholy . . . quality of his heroes.

"Perhaps it was his deep disdain for a world represented by bestial wars and the conflicts of modern industrial society, and for a life marked by loud machines, money grubbing and the quest for material comfort."

If so, the times, as perhaps the Army can divine from its dossiers, have certainly been a-changing. Vast and ever-growing flocks of Americans are reading Hesse now, youngish ones most of all. His work explodes across the land in paperback. There are one million of *Siddhartha* in print. They sold 360,000 of *Steppenwolf* in a single month. "His revival here has turned into a vogue, the vogue into a torrent," says one of the literati. Readers even write thank-you notes to Hesse's publishers. Fantastic. If it is not a movement, it is certainly a pilgrimage.

I got to it tardily, myself, certainly tardy in fashion's scheme of time, experiencing Hesse not in the mid-1960's, when he first began to draw a crowd, and not even in the late '60's, when the crowd had swollen to a throng. I took up with him just now, just last year, the year of John & Martha and Cambodia and Spiro and Kent State, a year when grand juries established the interesting principle of indicting the victims, and a year when Richard Milhous Nixon got stoned once again. It was, obviously, a very good year for traveling afar, wherever or however, so perhaps there was something providential in my timing, something timely in my yen. Like so many, I wondered why so many were taking the Hesse trip.

In any event, off I went, through the shadows and glint of being with Siddhartha, and then on—

—into *Steppenwolf,* watching Harry Haller, 48, the Steppenwolf, break out of the painful and arid prison into which vain intellect has locked him, listening to his anguished plaint—

A wild longing for strong emotions and sensations seethes in me, a rage against this toneless, flat, normal and sterile life. I have a mad impulse to smash something, a warehouse, perhaps, or a cathedral, or myself, to commit outrages, to pull off the wigs of a few revered idols . . . or to stand one or two representatives of the established order on their heads. For what I always hated and detested and cursed above all things was this contentment, this healthiness and comfort, this carefully preserved optimism of the middle classes, this fat . . . brood of mediocrity.

—and relishing his breakthrough, his wildly soaring thrust toward the lurid and kaleidoscopic completeness of himself, a head-bending orbiting of interior constellations via the Magic Theater, a labyrinthine fantasia, a phantasmagoria of the sensual and the passionate, the buried, the primal, all that poor Harry had blocked out all those years, denying the vast part of his being until he fell into the hands of twin-sexed Hermine and sensuous jazzman Pablo, they joining to lure him toward his deeper reaches, a long-buried but ever-moiling cosmos in which even his beloved Mozart laughs, and his beloved Goethe, too, mocking, shrieking laughter at the stringent intellect that had turned him into a dry and bitter prig, a suicidal mourner at life's scrumptious feast.

On went I, on into *Demian*, watching young Emil Sinclair, inspired by tough-minded Max Demian, the young man (or was he?) with the hypnotic and protean face—

". . . *it was not a boy's face but a man's; I [Sinclair] also felt that it was not entirely the face of a man either, but had something feminine about it, too. Yet the face struck me at that moment as neither masculine nor childlike, neither old nor young, but somehow a thousand years old, somehow timeless, bearing the scars of an entirely different history than we knew . . .*"

—that face, the timeless one, watching that Demian inspiring Sinclair to escape the shallow, plastic self that threatened him, the self with which the stuffy, middle-class culture would have bagged and sealed him in forever; and watching Sinclair make it, too, escape that doom, with the help of Demian's mother, Frau Eva, universal woman, a carnal-spectral figure whose pulsing, vibrant presence sends Sinclair's being out into the heavens amidst rocketing stars.

And so onward I, into *Peter Camenzind*, boxed in by a tiny Alpine village, a youth stifled and wind-grieved, pulsing with reverberant poetry, breaking away, flinging himself across the wide world, finding, of course, that he is alive, after all, but that the geographic cure is futile.

Thence into *Narcissus and Goldmund*, a longer tale, a riper figment. Like the others, its surface story is direct and clear. Good, close friends are the men of the title, yet different as can be. Narcissus, intellectual, devout, ascetic, joins, dwells and rises in the cloister, Mariabronn, and escapes the pain of existence at the cost of its juices. Goldmund, passionate, creative, impulsive, sometimes violent, departs the cloister, gorges on life. "Love and ecstasy were to him the only truly warming things that gave life its value." Goldmund wanders eerie, tumultuous landscapes that might be medieval or might not. Everywhere he finds the celebration of life, even in a plague-doomed country filled with the dead, even there amidst the grisly dying he finds this thing, finds survivors "grouped together by an excited, terrified lust for life, drinking and dancing and fornicating while death played the fiddle." As Frau Eva moved Sinclair, so a woman figure, universal mother, attends Goldmund. "She is everywhere," he says. And when, at the end, he dies in Narcissus' arms, Goldmund says: "But how will you die when your time comes, Narcissus, since you have no mother? Without a mother, one cannot love. Without a mother, one cannot die." Narcissus listens, and "Goldmund's last words burned like fire in his heart."

And so came the close of that story—but not of my pilgrimage and so onward I, traversing *The Journey to the East*, a little allegory of self-analysis, the self-search, psychoanalysis, if you will, an adumbration of that helter-skelter, halting, faltering process, the odyssey inward in which the trifle becomes crucial, the significant trivial, the familiar strange, the unexpected familiar and natural. I scampered through *Journey*, then on to Castalia, into *The Glass Bead Game*, cutting out of it without remorse, splitting as soon as I had read enough of it, and enough about it, to see that it was a lovingly and laboriously executed put-on and put-down of the world's vain and cloistered intellectual nit-pickers—the PhuDdy-duddies, I would call them. To Hesse, they are the inhabitants of a distant, future realm, Castalia, and they pass away their lives on earth playing the glass bead game, an interminable cerebral game, a game so abstruse and convoluted that nobody—not even Hesse—can describe it, a game the sublime absurdity of which is finally grasped by Joseph Knecht, the man who has become its foremost master. Knecht decides to relinquish that world of futile flapdoodle, and to do something useful, rewarding. He decides, specifically, to teach another young human being about existence, and to the doing of it he sacrifices his very life. Knecht, the hero's name, means servant. As a missionary's son, Hesse no doubt was familiar with the teachings of Jesus. Jesus taught that the chiefest among us would be called servant. So much for this elaborate parable, which has touched off many learned and erudite discussions by the PhuDdy-duddies.

While listening to Hesse, I listened, too, to others, those speaking of him. I listened to critics, to commentators, to extrapolators and exegetic masters, to fugitives from Castalia, to culture mongers, to oracles of the press and priests of the literati, to thumbsuckers, nailbiters and eye-browlifters, to put-downers and put-onners, listened to all and found all of them wondering, all of them pondering, as was I, professionally, why so many of the young were reading Hermann Hesse. I listened, they answered, some sneering at Hesse ("His art springs from an unshakably profound infatuation with adolescence"), some raising an aesthetic pinkie in dismay ("This is not literature; it is incense"), some aghast at his growing following ("one of the strangest cultural events of the present day"). Some astounded me, one pedagogue, particularly. He was writing in a scholarly journal, and he was telling his readers about Hesse, and he declared that "an outstanding example of the trivia of which most of Hesse's social observations consist" is "the tendency of modern civilized folk to waste time at playing bridge." Astounding. In my experience, Hesse's social observations in sum do a demolition job on Western civilization, its politics, its technology, its mode and substance, its entirety—including its stillborn pedagoguery. Conceivably this got in that scholarly fellow's turgid and recondite craw. Often, but not surprisingly, I found astral distances between what Hesse was saying and what others said he said.

I was, frankly, put off by the sneerers, the condescending ones who found Hesse too slight for their brand of maturity, that peculiar state of mind that issues "adolescent" as an epithet. (You find that state of mind in adults who ask children that familiar question. "What are you going to be when you grow up?"—that dumb and devastating question that tells the child he is nothing now, that carries the false suggestion that if he learns to do certain things—say, the things one must do to function as a fireman, mechanic, writer, lawyer, professor—he will somehow attain a state of being more worthwhile than that he possesses in life, mind and body.) I agreed with Webster Schott about Hesse: "His novels aren't adolescent fare. Their subtleties make work. Their simplicity belies galaxies of knowledge in motion—history, theology, psychology, philosophy... In Hesse's prose, youth ultimately reads the poetry of maturity." I agreed largely with the thoughtful studies of Hesse's biographer, Theodore Ziolkowski. Hesse, he says, is "a writer whose works anticipate with startling clarity the crucial dilemma of contemporary man in a dehumanized society." Of Hesse's appeal for the young, Ziolkowski adds:

"... Far from finding in Hesse merely a justification for dropping out, many sensitive readers today see in his works images for the most urgent problems that confront them: the quest for identity in a technological society, the search for a personal morality and a responsible individualism, the conflict between reflection and commitment... The sneering critics of the literary establishment reveal little but their own provincialism in their failure to understand the forces that move the [rising] generation."

And so to our epoch's big question again: just what moves the young? It persists and persists. From all sides come answers, every week, every month. We sniff them, refute them, confuse them, discard them. And we ask still again: Well, what moves the young? And all along the real answer is there scrolled out in lives. It unfolds by the year, in words and in deeds, rolled out before us. We hear but don't listen, we gape but don't see. What moves the young? The question strikes no fear in me, but I'm not going to venture an answer here, no sweeping synthesis. I frankly think the young are answering the query quite clearly themselves. They speak to me, in any event, but then I take life itself as a communication, each tick and quirk and twist and step. The person who brusquely turns a back toward me speaks as emphatically as the one who spells out go-to-hell. And I deem inattentive the parent who, morosely regarding a child that has rejected parental manners, morals, mores, politics, ideals, goals and companionship, complains peevishly that the child is not *communicating*. I don't believe that I could add a thing to that child's message, nor can I bring light to sightless parental eyes. I can console such a parent, however, prescribing *Siddhartha*, the tale of a man who turned his back on his father and later suffered rejection by his own son, nonetheless finding peace afterward, and wisdom. So it goes, and live and let live, I always say, and I do have an incurable weakness for those old cliches—you know: Judge not. Love thy enemy. Love thy neighbor as thyself. Know thyself. To thine own self be true. Find thyself by losing thyself.

Onward I, offward and onward circuitously, and back to Hesse, yet remaining with the young, the many young who are hearing him, and liking what they hear, and leaving us wondering. What could they possibly get out of him? Well, Hesse offers but a single thing. Hesse spent his whole life trying to know himself, losing himself to find himself, groping for wholeness, integrity, and often pained by the integrity he found. It compelled him to reject his native land because of its hideous penchant for war. All of Hesse's heroes, Siddhartha, Sinclair, Goldmund, burst out of old selves into new. Self-search is *all* he offers, the quest, the thrust toward awareness, the yearning for the meaning and dimensions of being.

To the Western Mind, such stuff is supposed to be remote, mystical, impenetrable even, lore out of the inscrutable East, occult land of illusory plains glistering under the incomprehensible All. They're fond of insinuating, some commentators, that the young are plunging right out of the rational world by soaking up Hesse, or taking up Zen, or drawing on the *I Ching*. I personally don't find that such a plunge takes me too far from home. Of course, I had the advantage of being reared in a sect that drilled me in esoteric things, convincing me that by being properly immersed in water, for example, I would be instantly reborn and would in fact live forever. They taught me that if I munched a bit of cracker and swallowed a tiny draught of grape juice, I would come into instant communion with the all-knowing power of existence—an all-knowing power, that, incidentally, was utterly singular while at the same time divided into three parts. They drilled in the teachings of the sect's ranking hero, and in this lore I learned, among other things, that I would gain myself by losing myself. Although my sect, as far as I recall, never used the *I Ching*, it taught that I could seek answers from the beyond itself by falling to my knees, by speaking to that singular great power in any or all of his three parts. I grew up, of course, in the remote and mystical and obscure and impenetrable American South, and was reared there in a congregation of the Southern Baptist Church. The preacher who finally convinced me when I was 12 that I was bound for eternal hell if I didn't march down that aisle—that eloquent and perspiring fellow coughed up some images that would have made Steppenwolf quail, man, sending him stumbling not into the Magic Theater but right down that quivering aisle, with all the sweet ladies of the church, and some of the men, too, merchants and bankers and lawyers, singing *Just as I Am*. Perhaps the East is not as far from the West as some of our public monitors assume.

Perhaps, in truth, the twain have met. But now, brooding on Hesse and the young, I hang on the line a mere prejudice of my golden middle years. I confess that I view human existence as a singular thing (though it explodes in myriad expressions), and the earth as a singular globe, on which west leads to east, and up leads to down. Rationality passes over the threshold to lunacy. To safeguard life, man rationally perfects the means to exterminate it. To serve him, man ingeniously devises a rational technology that masters him. I watch it with perpetual wonder but infrequent astonishment. The circuitry of man's little globe has become very interesting. The lights of mankind can be turned off as quickly by a finger in Moscow as in Washington. In the shadow of the works of rationality, it is reasonable for men to seek joy beyond reason.

So I accept as sweet sanity the self-searching of the young. It seems reasonable that Hesse has discovered them. I suspect it is time for us to see that life moves the young and cease asking what moves them as though it were secret. Instead of wondering what moves the young, we should wonder from what they are moving. What indeed could impel their quest except what they see of life and man? And here they see habitual rationalizations of poisons and evils that blight the earth, menacing life itself.

In a recent piece on the psychoanalyst C. G. Jung, psychiatrist David Elkind pointed out that Jung's life observations were prophetic of the stirrings of young people today, and of other rising tides in men's minds, of their interest in "Eastern" lore, in Buddhism, in their pilgrimages away from stale selves that smack of death. Jung taught that man approaches a sense of wholeness only as he exercises all his psychic functions, thinking and feeling, sensation and intuition. Individuals neglecting any suffer, and so do cultures. In its obsessive rationalistic conceit the West had gone too far, Jung felt. Now some souls are shaking free. As Elkind summarized:

" . . . in Western society, the deification of reason, of industrialization and technology together with the intellectualization of religion, has progressively alienated modern man from his inner world and from his feeling function. Jung believed that the rapid growth of contemporary interest in the *I Ching* . . . in spiritualism, in astrology, in psychology and in Eastern religions is a natural reaction to Western man's exaggerated extraverted thinking function. Cultures, no less than individuals, can lack wholeness and completeness . . . Likewise, today's youths are generally disdainful of the dead symbols of institutional religion, but are intensely interested in spiritual matters, in finding new ways to explore inner experience and in finding new symbols to guide their explorations—hence their interest in eastern religions, whose symbols seem to be alive in . . . that they retain an air of mystery."

Jung and Hesse, friends in life, were twins in their view of the purpose of man. "Man," said the psychoanalyst, "should live according to his own nature; he should concentrate on self-knowledge and then live in accordance with the truth about himself." Hesse wrote tales of his quest. Jung worked out his hypothesis, his map of the psyche. Jung's was the concept of the *persona*, that visible self, foremost in the consciousness, that fabrication of roles that you play, as a son, a pupil, a merchant, a lawyer, a soldier—roles required by the culture that invents this "you." Beneath that lurks a *shadow*, Jung believed, a real being of your own, repressed but lurching forth now and then, unpredictable, often unacceptable, yet there, an active thing. Under that, buried deep, beyond consciousness, seethes the *animus*, the *anima*, in the man or the woman, the inner being, beyond direct conscious reach, yet erupting through in dreams, in fantasies, in one's projections. To Jung, putting it roughly, the way to self-knowledge, to wholeness, to *individuation*, he called it, is the expansion of awareness of these often slippery elements of the psyche, an awareness leading to harmonious acceptance of all of your parts—along with a balanced exercise of all psychic functions—thinking, feeling, sensation, intuition. The Jungian trip would be mind-bending.

And so, of course, is the Hesse trip. The path is quite the same. A primer on Jung would be the best preface to any Hesse tale. In each, the hero follows the Jungian way, struggling from dissatisfaction with the persona, increasing awareness of submerged shadow beings within, into the quest, the grapplings, the confusions, the symbols of the animus-anima swarming to the fore, swarming among those other Jungian things, the archetypal beings that dwell in what Jung called the *collective unconscious*. As I reread Hesse's tales, the surface stories, the plots, shrank away, as eventually the singularity of the characters did. I began to fathom that in each tale, *all* the characters exist only in the psyche of the protagonist, and beyond that, that all of these exist only as characters from the psyche of Hermann Hesse. So finally the trip was a sojourn to a mind.

At the finish, it was an exposure not to Literature, not to The Lyrical Novel, but simply a long listening to the fanciful words of a man long gone, another being, a human creature who passed just as you and I are passing, briefly here, swiftly across the face of earth.

Hermann Hesse was born in a Black Forest village called Calw. As a child, he suffered under pious parents who tried to force on him a self he knew he was not. As a man, he exiled himself from Germany, detesting its militarism. He married. He begat a child. He divorced, married again. Along the way, he suffered a nervous breakdown. He was healed through psychoanalysis ministered by a disciple of Jung. Once he made a pilgrimage to India, returned, settled in Switzerland. Life passed on. He tended his garden and wrote letters to friends and studied his books and wrote down his tales. He grew old. He died. Behind him he left his words. I do not wish to bury them in an abstract category.

I took the Hesse trip in my own way, letting go, surrendering to that marvelous and improbable human thing, the opening of one mind to another, mine to Hesse's, opening up and listening, listening to the long-gone speak to the now, listening for the twang of elemental tensions rightly strung, gathering in figments, figments of his swarming in among figments of mine, marvelous.

Stuff of a mind spawned in the Kaiser's Germany visiting the stuff of a mind spawned in Bilbo's South, mindstuff melding with mindstuff: Siddhartha meets Flem Snopes, Steppenwolf in the sorghum patch, C. G. Jung among the hymn singers, Atman goes to Sunday school, Aunt Jemima pops out of a cornmeal bag and says *auf wiedersehen*, the *I Ching* meets a talking possum, and more: twin-sexed Hermine comes to the garden alone while the dew is still on the roses, and here comes Goldmund:

. . . ever-horny Goldmund hovering up out of his weird passionscape to swoop down past the miasmal gumbo of the hoot-owled bottomland and up among the hilly pines, and his first halting, exalting seduction melds with groping young lust in the towering trees, soaring, creaking, moaning pines, late one afternoon, in August, long, long ago. No: just now, now when the late sun blades down through the pines, sun sheering down in planes of eerie ochre light to dismember forever young lusters intuiting a time out of mind, mind out of time, intuiting the time when man to his astonishment discovered lust turning into love and so ran scampering

and jabbering through the vaulted trees questing words that might tell something of this astonishing and soaring new thing,

And then Goethe enters laughing, laughing as never he laughed in his plastercasted presence atop the mantel, the mantel of the library, the library of the house, the house of my grandfather-the-lawyer, the house where I grew up, in Bilbo's South, in Mississippi, far from the Kaiser's Germany, far from the Black Forest where Hesse grew up: marvelous, I thought, that Goethe, coming to laugh cosmically at Steppenwolf, could disgorge from my mindstuff the moment in greengold December when I walked into that library and saw as usual Goethe on the double mantelpiece, his little plaster likeness, and saw the others—Shakespeare, Homer, and, of all things, Woodrow Wilson, whom my grandfather resembled—and saw, then, my brother, at 17 two years my senior, standing there remote and spectral in dimness, the light turned viridescent by late sun pressing in through green shades, saw him and heard him say, matter-of-factly, in his way, *"Daddy died today,"* and waited for him to say more, which he did, explaining. "We got a telegram from his wife," which made me wonder, standing there in the greenish light, careening in a gathering gloom, staring blankly up at Shakespeare and Homer and Woodrow Wilson and mirthless Goethe, wondering, because I didn't even know he had got another wife. Now Goethe laughs, and I do, too, and I am grateful that Hesse spoke to me, as life so often does, unexpectedly, to us fleeting tenants of this gorgeous planet, this demeaned little ball that shows such shimmering promise to the moon.

—LOOK, February 23, 1971

The '70s: A Time Of Pause

1978

Once gone, and often before, every decade migrates into the vocabulary of folklore. There it persists as a sort of handy hieroglyph for conjuring up popular memories of a time. So it is that "the '20s," as a phrase, evokes not only *The Great Gatsby* but more social lore than the entire text of the novel. Similarly, to allude to the '30s, the '40s, the '50s or the '60s is to speak volumes. In contrast, the '70s have not, so to speak, learned to talk.

The waning decade has remained elusive, unfocused, a patchwork of dramatics awaiting a drama. Here on the brink of the '80s, it would still be risky to guess what people will mean when they speak of the '70s ten years from now. Why have these times seemed so indefinite?

There are doubtless many reasons. An odd but important one is that the '60s lasted too long. As folklore, decades seldom observe the calendar's nice limits. The '20s actually began with the adoption of Prohibition; the '30s, launched by the 1929 crash, did not end until 1941, when the U.S. entered the big war. The election of Dwight Eisenhower as President in 1952 began the time consistently, if imperfectly, remembered as the quiet '50s. The furies and griefs that are recalled as the essence of the '60s began not in 1960 but at the death of John Kennedy. Then came that brutal ransacking of the national spirit that did not even pause at the end of 1969 but continued through the disillusionments of Watergate. The 60s did not really let go until Richard Nixon resigned.

So it may be that the '70s, having started late, have not been going on long enough to give clear shape to whatever they are finally to be. At first, they could scarcely be recognized except by what they were not. Mainly, they were not the '60s. To an exhausted, convalescent society this was a relief but also disconcerting. It was not easy, even with Jerry Ford in the White House, to begin watching for pratfalls instead of apocalypses. Still, by the time Jimmy Carter tried to whip up a moral crusade for energy conservation, much of the country seemed to have perfected the knack of shrugging off the alarms of crisis. It was easy to read that mood as indifference, but it is more reasonable to suppose the country just needed a rest.

It did not come to a dead standstill, however, and the record of the trends and tendencies of the brief post-'60s period has become clear enough. So has the fact that the record is shot through with perplexing contradictions. Any attentive observer could jot down a fast thumbnailer of the '70s so far:

The voters were apathetic; no, they were outraged at taxes and mobilized to demand reform. People had given up on the capacities of government; no, citizens everywhere were forming diligent factions and forcing government's hand on one issue and another. The individual had learned he could not change anything; no, so many individuals had learned they could shake things up in court that there was a litigation crisis.

More: Society had slumped into a posture of cynical disbelief; no, the search for spiritual illumination was epidemic and had grown so fervent that it was endangering the state-church separation. The moral permissiveness achieved in the '60s was ripening into generalized decadence: no, not only was fidelity growing fashionable once again, but television was even cutting back on sex and violence for fear of *losing* the mass audience.

Clearly this social flux consisted more of motion than of movement. The women's liberation movement may turn out to be profoundly epochal, but neither it nor any other trend gripped or provoked the nation as did, say, the now quiescent civil rights crusade. Surely no single label or slogan could possibly embrace such a diffuse drama, and efforts to encapsulate these times in a single-shot insight have been quite unconvincing.

Some have called it the "apathetic age," but to accept this is to be blind to boundless activity by innumerable social and political groups. In its farewell issue, *New Times* depicted this as a "decadent" age; yet the magazine itself, though born out of the sensibilities of the '60s, went out sounding a faintly puritanical note that was proof that not everything had been infected by decadence. American journalism has always been inspired more by the Mafia than by the Gray Ladies. Moreover, it has a recurring weakness for the kind tunnel vision that imagines a glimpse into Plato's Retreat reveals the daydreams of the inhabitants of Texarkana. So it is useful to remember the warp of many impressions of the '70s that have gained currency. Some result from the tendency to mistake the new and exotic for the prevalent and enduring.

Many commentators, all too many, have followed the lead of New Journalist Tom Wolfe and accepted the '70s as the "me decade." Wolfe's term has been useful, but anyone who imagines that it is definitive has swallowed a dose of glib chic whole. The discovery of the insuperable self-centeredness of human nature did not await the '70s. Neither did the national habit of self-improvement, which was going strong when Public Man Ben Franklin was its high priest. Broadly, the premise of the "me decade" view is that great numbers of people are disdaining society to pursue existence as narcissistic massage buffs, om-sayers, encounter groupies and peacocks. The type is to be found, true, but the number seems very small. A thousand times as many Americans are to be found at any time—around hospitals, churches, offices, schools, neighborhoods—all as lost as ever in the volunteerism that has been a striking phenomenon of the national character since Tocqueville came meandering about. Thank God he did not get his information from the crowd at Elaine's.

Anyhow, self-improvement is not incompatible with sociability. Even joggers have been known to donate to the United Fund. Such matters ought also to be spread on the record—but without any intent to identify the '70s as the "civic decade." It has, unquestionably, been a confused time, neither here nor there, neither the best nor worst of times, as free of a predominant theme as of a singular direction. Maybe the reason is not even visible. Maybe the little energy left over from the '60s got mostly spent, in secret, on assimilating and liquidating the traumas and griefs of that overlong epoch. If so, then perhaps the most memorable thing about the '70s has been simply that, as Stanford Sociologist Seymour Martin Lipset observed, "nothing disastrous is happening." Such a historical pause may not at the moment seem worth remembering—but it will as soon as disaster drops among us again.

—*TIME*, December 25, 1978

Looking For Tomorrow (And Tomorrow)

1982

Prediction is very difficult, especially about the future.
—Niels Bohr

Asked to make sense of Pharaoh's dreams about fat and lean cows and plump and withered ears of corn, Joseph took them as signs of coming events. The *Book of Genesis* records his forecast: "Behold, there come seven years of great plenty throughout all the land of Egypt. And there shall arise after them seven years of famine." Pharaoh was so pleased to get a fix on the future that he made Joseph the ruler of Egypt. If Joseph materialized now, politics would make it hard for him to get his old job back, but with his proven foresight he would soon find work.

Today people crave to know what lies ahead at least as much as they did in Pharaoh's time. Probably more. Modern times have created a perpetual bull market in futures. Society spends so much time looking ahead that the present sometimes seems entirely forgotten. Corporations live for the next quarter; ordinary citizens exist to fulfill next summer's vacation budget. Governments at all levels stay mired in hassles over how things will turn out.

All the tools of technology are brought into the effort to see around the distant bend in the river. Thus planning has grown into a full-fledged industry in the 20th century. The trend is striking, but even more impressive is how little mankind has progressed in its efforts to plumb the future since those days of prophetic dreams.

Still, scarcely a salient public issue comes up that does not demand at least an effort to read the future. How long will the recession go on? Whither Central America? Will the energy crisis ever come back? Will space become a theater for military action? Society flourishes or languishes by guessing the drift of things. If it had guessed right about consumer trends a few years ago, the auto industry might not be in such a sorry state. But in that industry, as Chrysler's chairman Lee Iacocca put it, "you make a decision and then wait three years to get the stuff kicked out of you." Congress has such a hunger to know coming trends that it requires the President to project budget deficits five years ahead—an exercise to whose futility Ronald Reagan recently attested. Said Reagan: "I have to be honest with you and tell you that while I have to project . . . I don't believe what I'm saying."

Even professional planners are learning (from bruising themselves on the future's impenetrable surface) to put only qualified belief in their own findings. Says Roy Amara, president of the Institute for the Future in Menlo Park, California: "Anything that you forecast is by definition uncertain." Thomas J. Watson, founder of IBM, would surely have agreed, and perhaps not too long after forecasting "I think there is a world market for about five computers." Leon Eplan, ex-president of the American Institute of Planners and now chairman of the city planning department at the Georgia Institute of Technology, says that the planning profession has finally been chastened by the uncertainty of technological change. Says Eplan: "When I started my career, I was predicting 20 years into the future. I never do that any more."

Economic forecasters have taken a conspicuous bloodying in recent years for their habitual failures. They suffer even more than usual difficulty when they work for the Government, according to Rudolph Penner, who was chief economist in the budget office under President Gerald Ford. Says Penner: "One of the great problems is not so much that economists are not good at forecasting but that the politicians insist on very rosy numbers." Indeed, most politicians may secretly agree with David Stockman's private theory about national planning: "None of us really understands what's going on with all these numbers."

If looking ahead—planning, predicting—were only a matter of technique, there would doubtless be simple technical explanations for the repetitious failures. But the great uncontrollable element in the human future is just that—its humanity, profoundly quirky and ultimately unpredictable. Energy analysts expecting sustained oil shortages failed to realize that people would start conserving as dramatically as they did. Many marketing forecasters underestimated the buying trends of the 1970s because they assumed prices and income controlled spending. Recalls Robert Gough, senior vice president of Data Resources, Inc. in Lexington, Massachusetts, consumers spent like mad because they expected ever higher prices. Says Gough: "What was missing in our equations was this price expectation phenomenon."

The human factor, above all others has made the words unintended consequences into a buzz phrase among professional planners. And "unintended consequence" is simply a euphemism for what people actually do with what is given. The carefully planned federal highway system, for instance, was not intended to promote suburban development while draining vitality from the cities—but it accomplished just that. Says Louis Masotti, professor of political science and urban affairs at Northwestern University: "Such unintended consequences go a long way toward explaining the sorry state of cities today."

There is no respectable argument against efforts to plan. The practicality of looking ahead has been more than proved by the results of occasional failures to do so. One useful symbol of inadequate planning might be the S-curve bridge that Chicago had to build when its north Lake Shore Drive failed to end at the same place as its south Lake Shore Drive. Even so, the fact that planning can help does not mean that a constant preoccupation with tomorrow (and tomorrow and tomorrow) is beneficial.

It is not. There are reasons why folklore and religious teachings warn people against giving too much of their attention to the future. Taking too much thought for the morrow can, in fact, insulate a person far too much from the reality of the present—and the real nature of the future. It is not what futurologists make it out to be—some palpable thing rushing toward society, projectile-like, out of the void. "The future is smashing into us so forcefully that it can no longer be ignored," say Edward Cornish and others of the World Future Society in one of their books. They add: "A maelstrom of social change has engulfed the world." If so, what has engulfed the world is not something out of a menacing tomorrow but only yesterday coming to fruition.

Actually, the future does not exist except as a concept, a cosmic wisp of possibility. How people view it can make big differences. What befalls society around the bend in the river will not come hurtling out of space (weather excepted) but will have arisen out of today. "The present," as Philosopher Gottfried Wilhelm Leibniz put it, "is pregnant with the future." The highest prudence consists not of looking ahead but of giving the best care to the burgeoning and, for better or worse, fruitful moment at hand.

—*TIME*, April 26, 1982

ABOUT THE AUTHOR

Frank Trippett was born in 1926 and grew up in Aberdeen, Mississippi. He attended Mississippi College, Duke University, and the University of Mississippi. Mr. Trippett's first job as a journalist was with the Meridian (Mississippi) *Star*. He fell in love with journalism, which he later called, "that trade that was designed in heaven for those of us who are unsuited for useful employment." Mr. Trippett worked for the Fredericksburg (Virginia) *Free Lance-Star*, and was the Capital Bureau Chief for the St. Petersburg (Florida) *Times* before joining NEWSWEEK magazine as an Associate Editor in 1961. He was a Senior Editor at *LOOK* magazine and a Senior Writer and essayist for *TIME* magazine. His writing won awards from the National Headliner Club, the National Bar Association and the American Political Science Association. Mr. Trippett is the author of the nonfiction books *The States, United They Fell* (1967) and *The First Horsemen* (1974), as well as the novel *Child Ellen* (1975). His essays have been anthologized in numerous college writing textbooks. This book is the first comprehensive collection of his essays, spanning over a quarter of a century of "hymning and hawing" about America. Mr. Trippett and his wife Betty lived, and raised their four children, in Larchmont, New York, until his death at the age of 71 in 1998.

"Frank Trippett was an unbounded character—a dangerous and lovely guy. He was one of the really mind-blowing talents of his generation as a journalist, essayist, poet, story teller and as a man rambling about town. His wit was as quick as his left and he could open your eyes to things unseen. Or, maybe, he'd give you a deep, slow chuckle and make you say, "Yeah. Yeah." He always dealt with the most dangerous commodity around—truth. And the consequences just didn't bother him. Frank's gone. You can't visit with him. Read his work."

—Bill Emerson/former Editor-in-Chief,
The Saturday Evening Post

"I read Frank Trippett's novel *Child Ellen* and found it moving and full of Faulknerian insights. His essays were models of stylish restraint. When I ran *TIME*'s book review section he once wrote a piece about a town in France that had saved every one of its Jews during the Occupation. He wrote that it was a case of goodness seeming to come out of nowhere, and that all humans were capable of it, sometimes when they were least aware. This, it seems to me, was Frank's greatest contribution—that he made us find our better selves."

—Stefan Kanfer/Author,
former *TIME* "Books" Editor

"Frank Trippett, one of the finest men I've known, was also one of the liveliest, funniest, and wisest writers. In his essays, you hear a touch of the preacher, a lot of the storyteller and satirist. He was an anecdotalist of great gifts. What we loved about Frank and his work was his combination of humor and indignant decency, a sweetness illuminated by high intelligence."

—Lance Morrow/Essayist